TAO TE CHING

Chinese Medicine

The Acupuncture Comprehensive Prescriptive Index

Dictionary of Acupuncture Terms, Concepts and Points

Acupuncture: The Special Function Points

Acupuncture with Your Fingers

The Macro-Acupuncture Manual

The Acupuncture Certification Review Book of Questions and Answers

Acupoint Exercises for the Six Senses

Music

Music in the Round

Accompanied Rounds

Rhythm: Activities and Instruments

Books for Children

When I Met Robin

Shoes, Pennies and Rockets

Lenore and the Wonder House

Games to Sing and Play

The Dale Recorder Method

LAO TZU

TAO TE CHING

A New Translation & Commentary

by

RALPH ALAN DALE

Ed.D., Ph.D., A.P., Dipl.Ac.

Photographs by John Cleare

BARNES
& NOBLE
NEW YORK

2005 Barnes & Noble Publishing

ISBN-13: 978-0-7607-4998-2
ISBN-10: 0-7607-4998-1

Printed and bound in China

7 9 11 13 15 14 12 10 8 6

Dedication

To Lao Tzu who, through his courage, imagination, intuition, insight and wisdom, conceived of the Great Integrity (Tao).

To the millions of tribal people who lived in the Great Integrity, thereby proving to us that it is as natural to our species just as it is, and always has been, the only way of life ever known to every other species.

To the hundreds of millions of human beings who have been victimized by our loss of the Great Integrity during the era we euphemistically call civilization, and to the countless species that were sacrificed at the altars of our civilizations.

To the astonishing technologies that civilizations created as bi-products of scarcity relative to need, and whose modus vivendi was and still continues to be greed. But these technologies have taken such qualitative leaps that now, paradoxically, they have become fundamental to our potential to realize planetary abundance, and so the means to 'anachronize' the very system of greed that originally generated them.

To the hundreds of thousands of courageous visionaries who have dedicated their lives to the rebirth of the Great Integrity during the myriad centuries when, at most, it could enlighten our hearts and dreams, but could not yet be achieved as an alternative way of life.

To the tens of millions of us who today are joining hands across the planet, committed to the conscious evolution of the Great Integrity Renaissance whose time has finally come.

To the billions of future human beings who will live the Great Integrity in dimensions far beyond our wildest dreams, and who will forever be appreciative of Lao Tzu, of the tribal people, of civilizations' victims, of our ultimate technologies, of the courageous visionaries, and of those of us who today are so fortunate to be the midwives of the Great Transformation.

"And to my wife, Hendrina. Our unconditional love has fueled my personal inspiration to write this book, piercing years of armoring, and opening my heart to the Great Integrity."

Contents

Foreword

BY
BARBARA MARX HUBBARD
AUTHOR AND PRESIDENT OF THE FOUNDATION FOR CONSCIOUS EDUCATION

The spiral of our evolutionary progress is turning back in time to reconnect with the great sage Lao Tzu. In his understanding of the Tao, we find vital guidance and a natural way for us to realign with the implicate enfolded order in evolution. He stands before us, a beneficent presence, gently reminding us to become aware of transformational patterns and to practice conscious evolution.

The Great Integrity is his beautiful description of the whole connected field of de-ideologized reality out of which our liberating alternatives are arising. He is a post post modern teacher, standing beyond the artificial constructions and deconstructions of current thought, serving as our guardian and guide of the perennial wisdom of humanity. He calls to us to re-enter the harmony of nature, now as sovereign whole persons. No longer children seeking external deities, or self-centered materialists seeking power over nature and each other, we become co-creators with the great creating process itself, integral active agents of the Great Integrity.

About two thousand years before Lao Tzu's time, marked the momentous transition from the earlier phase of human history — when we lived in relative harmony with nature, caring for each other by necessity — to the coercive civilizations of the past five thousand years. At this transformational point, agriculture gave us the capacity to create a surplus by forcing the majority to enrich a minority which usurped the power to control society. The egalitarian social structures of the far longer human past were shattered. It was no longer a biological necessity to care for each other. Rather, there was an advantage for some to gain superiority over others. We moved, in Riane Eisler's phrase, from a partnership model to a dominator model. Masters and slaves, wealthy and poor, armies and weapons of mass destruction developed. However, the benefits of this last phase were surely great, culminating in science, individuality and — for some — freedom, abundance and education. None the less, in our time, the dysfunctional ties of this form of social structure have now become apparent.

If we continue, even one more generation, over-populating, polluting, warring and ever-widening the gap between the rich and the poor, we see the evolutionary "handwriting on the wall". We can destroy our life support systems and even make our species extinct.

As Einstein said, we cannot solve our problems in the same state of consciousness in which we created them. The ancient teaching of Lao Tzu now becomes the new necessity. Modern evolutionary thinkers, writers and activists are seeking to reconnect with the patterns in natural systems, beginning to learn how to become co-evolutionary with these patterns which Lao Tzu called the *Tao* and which Dr. Dale translates as the *Great Integrity*.

Lao Tzu is a masterful guide, and Ralph Alan Dale has given us the precise interpretation that we need so that we may apply this teaching to our vital quest for co-evolution and co-creation. Lao Tzu's time has come, and this book is a magnificent, clear, poetic rendering of the ancient truth now reborn in our age. It is as if Lao Tzu himself has guided the understanding of Dr. Dale, whose reverence and brilliance shines through every word.

Introduction

The *Tao Te Ching*[1] is an ancient Chinese book composed of only five thousand characters and written perhaps as early as the sixth century BCE,[2] by Lao Tzu, the legendary father of Taoism.

For centuries, this small book of Lao Tzu's sayings had no name. It was like the Tao itself that is introduced right at the outset:

> The Tao that can be told
> is not the universal Tao.
> The name that can be named
> is not the universal name.[3]

More than four centuries after Lao Tzu was supposed to have lived, Si-Ma Qian (Ssu-Ma Ch'ien) observed that the book was divided into two parts. Thereafter people began to refer to these two parts as *Tao* and *Te*. Still later, the book was divided into eighty-one sections. Verses 1-37 are called the *Tao* section because Verse 1 begins with the word, *Tao*. Verses 38-81 are called the *Te* section because Verse 38 begins with the word *Te*. Then the word *Ching* was added to the title. Ching means *Ancient Text* or *Classic*.

Tao means *path*. For Lao Tzu, it signifies not just any path, but the specific path to living in concordance with the unity of the universe. According to Lao Tzu, it is the nature of nature to issue from an inextricable relationship of every part to the whole. To live life in accord with the Tao is to be in harmony with all others, with the environment and with one's self. It is to live in synchronicity with processes, and to be completely authentic, sincere, natural and innocent. The word *integrity* embraces all these characteristics. Tao also implies the inexhaustible greatness and wonderfulness of the universe and every part of it.[4] All these propositions provide what modern science would call a theory of the nature of the universe. I therefore translate Tao as the *Theory of the Great Integrity*. Te means *virtue* or the practice of the Tao, and Ching, as already indicated above, means a *classic book* or *guide*. I therefore translate the *Tao Te Ching* as *A Guide to the Theory and Practice of the Great Integrity*.

The *Tao Te Ching* is one of the most widely translated books in the world. During the past 2,400 years there may have been as many as 1,400 different interpretations with perhaps 700 extant.[5] This book continues to fascinate people throughout the world. Why?

I believe it is because the *Tao Te Ching* confronts and offers an alternative to our schizoid ways of thinking, feeling and behaving. Every section appeals to an innate holistic wisdom that our innermost being has longed for during all these past so-called civilized millennia – sometimes consciously, often unconsciously. Lao Tzu's words invite us to transcend words since words are used as the rationalizations of the tyrannies that we have established over each other.[6] He offers us what in his time were alternative utopian pathways to a more harmonious life. Today, in this dawn of the twenty-first century, the Great Integrity presents itself as a practical and achievable goal and perhaps as the only alternative to our own species extinction.

THE PARADOX OF LANGUAGE

Right at the beginning, Lao Tzu invites us to transcend words:

> *In the infancy of the universe,*
> *there were no names.*
> *Naming fragments the mysteries of life*
> *into ten thousand things and*
> *their manifestations.*[7]

But how does one take issue with the world of words without using words? By being rather than by arguing. That, in fact, was Lao Tzu's way. He probably never wrote this book because polemics was the very target of his advocacy.[8] More likely, many generations of his disciples and followers summarized his philosophy of life in these metaphoric fragments which sing the literary music of the right brain,[9] the transcendence of language through unordinary language.

Because paradox is the principal mode of Lao Tzu's thought processes, and because it is the nature of the Chinese language, especially ancient Chinese, to be poetic, I have rendered these 81 sections as verses, although the original is written more like Chinese prose than poetry. Moreover, how else than through poetry can one employ the left brain to transcend itself? How else can one criticize logical thinking without using logic? And how else does one merge yin and yang[10] whose very nature expresses polarization?

Above all, it is not Lao Tzu's way to preach. He gently reminds us that preaching is a judgmental activity that negates the Great Integrity. But the very act of raising the flag of the Great Integrity

is itself an act of preaching, one of the inherent paradoxes of the *Tao Te Ching*.

But the opposite of disputation and logic is not randomness and irrationality. I have attempted in these translations to preserve a subject focus while immersing each verse in the paradoxes that are at the heart of Lao Tzu's thought. The translations have deliberately avoided entrapment in either the prison of logic or in a hodge-podge of disconnected thoughts.

It is the paradox of every poet to have to transcend the logical function of language through language. It is a higher level of paradox when the very content of the poetry is dedicated to this transcendence. The ultimate consistency of Lao Tzu's wisdom is for us to communicate through silence, but consistency is also a negation of his wisdom. Since the *Tao Te Ching* itself is a communication through words, the very act of writing or reading this book is an affirmation that words are not really the enemy. The enemy is the perversion of words to manipulate the disadvantaged, and their further perversion to rationalize the consequent inhumanities of these manipulations.[11] On the contrary, the words of Lao Tzu point us toward our liberation from inequities and injustices, that is, toward the Great Integrity.

TAO – THE GREAT INTEGRITY

What is the Tao? It is the oneness of all reality. According to Lao Tzu, the Tao or Great Integrity is the origin and nature of the Universe.[12] It is the way of life for all species on our planet, including human beings living in most tribal societies.

> *In ancient times*
> *the people knew the Great Integrity*
> *in all its subtlety and profundity.*[13]

TABLE 1
DIFFERENTIATING THE CHARACTERISTICS OF THE
LEFT AND RIGHT CEREBRAL HEMISPHERES
(In Right Handed People)

ASPECT	LEFT CEREBRAL HEMISPHERE	RIGHT CEREBRAL HEMISPHERE
Activity	Doing/Accomplishing	Being
Art	Logical/Commercial	Emotional/Aesthetic
Behavior	Predictable/Repeatable	Unpredictable/Spontaneous
Communication—Mode	Speech/Language	Imagery/Music/Dance
Communication —Function	Structure/Control/Rationalize	Feel /Love
Consciousness—Character	Individual	Social
Consciousness—Psychoanalysis	Ego/Superego	Id/Collective unconscious
Consciousness—State	Beta/Waking	Alpha/Delta/Theta/ "Altered"
Discipline	Sciences/Mathematics	Arts
Ecology	Alienated	Integral
Evolution (Phylogenic/Ontogenic)	Later Development	Earlier Development
Focus	Parts	Whole
Intention	Planned/Calculated	Unplanned
Investigative Method	Scientific	Magical/Metascientific
Language	Logic/Prose	Paradox/Ambiguity/Poetry
Learning—Form	Abstract	Concrete
Learning—Method	Memorization/Analysis	Experience
Learning—Substance	Knowledge	Knowing
Learning—Time	Gradual	Instantaneous
Meaning	Literal	Metaphoric
Medicine	Allopathic	Naturopathic
Mode of Thought	Analytic/Manipulative	Intuitive
Perception	Objective/Sensory Information	Subjective/Sensory Reactivity
Recreation	Intellectual	Sports/Meditation
Polarity	Positive/Active/Yang	Negative/Passive/Yin
Recognition of Individuals	By Name	By Face
Psychic Orientation	Intellectual/Moral	Emotional/Spiritual
Psychic Pathology	Emotional Victimizer Rationalization Alienation Logic Without Wholeness Polarization of Reason	Emotional Victim Irrationality Emotional Confusion Wholeness Without Logic Polarization of Emotions
Psychotherapy	Psychoanalysis	Affective Therapies
Religious Orientation	Sectarian dogma	Experiential
Social Orientation	Aggressive/Competitive	Peaceful/Cooperative
Space Perception	Uses Quantitative Measurements	Uses Kinesthetics

Later, since the advent of civilizations, we human beings lost the Great Integrity, exchanging our natural harmony with the universe for ego-oriented life styles. However, Lao Tzu expresses confidence that we will one day recover the Great Integrity.

Paradoxically, Lao Tzu states that we will recover the Great Integrity without trying. So how is it possible for us to transform ourselves without trying to do so? There are two components of this paradox: The first is subjective and applies both to Lao Tzu's time as well as our own. The second is a unique objective aspect of our radical evolution in this twenty-first century.

(1) Lao Tzu doesn't mean by "not trying" that we should accept our present unhappy condition. He identifies trying with forcing. To act without trying means to act without coercion. He offers *being* as an alternative to *trying*. The implication is that even before we transform the world in accordance with our age-old dream, we can transcend our indoctrination and life styles by being – or at least beginning to be – that totally human person that our species nature craves. Lao Tzu advises us to have the courage to begin to live in the future now as a means to our own transcendence.[14]

(2) This ability *to be* before we *become*, is much more possible for us today, than it was for people in Lao Tzu's time, because, in a sense, it is we, not Lao Tzu's contemporaries, who live in the evolutionary epoch of transition. Until now, in every civilization, relative economic scarcity has defined the objective conditions that have chained us to a way of life that violates our own natures as well as the nature of nature. But we twenty-first century-ites have already discovered one of the fundamental prerequisites for the full actualization of our human species potentials by having created the technology to live in a planetary economy of abundance. The proviso, of course, is that we utilize this technology productively to fulfill the needs of all people on the planet instead of squandering it on intraspecies conflicts and gross inequitable distributions.

In fact, the contradiction between having achieved a qualitatively new level of technology and clinging anachronistically to our old social relations defines our main problem today. Instead of utilizing our new technological capacities to create a world of abundance, we turn them into Frankensteins of mass destruction – vandalizing nature as well as our own material creations and ourselves. Indeed, we are already at the gates of technological liberation while our social, economic and political institutions and our spirituality live in a cultural limbo, oblivious that some of the main preconditions for our evolutionary transformation have already been achieved.

THE THREE ASPECTS OF LIBERATION.

There is a developmental process through which we may become liberated from our limitations and distortions, and through which we can begin to enter the alternative world of the Great Integrity. We can identify three interdependent aspects: 1) Detoxifying the mental-emotional-spiritual garbage that we all inherit, 2) Returning to our own humanity and 3) Transforming our institutions and ourselves to fully realize our human potential. These three aspects are metaphorically recounted in the following story.[15]

A few travelers were passing a Sufi monastery. Their curiosity led them to look through the open door to see what was happening. People were screaming, jumping, freaking out and, it seemed, just going completely mad. In the midst of all this chaos, the Master was sitting calmly and silently. The travelers said to each other that they thought that monasteries are where people go to attain enlightenment. However, here the Master seems to have attracted insanity. He also seems to be out of touch since he sits quietly meditating, apparently oblivious to the chaos going on all around him. The travelers left, shaking their heads in disbelief.

After a few months, these travelers once again came through that same town and passed the monastery. They again looked through the open door, expecting to see the raving maniacs. To their utter amazement, they observed the very same people, silently sitting in meditation. The contrast to their first observation seemed incomprehensible. Once again they left shaking their heads in disbelief.

A few months passed. Again these travelers returned to that town and, of course, were curious to see what was happening in the monastery. They tiptoed to the open door, and now found to their surprise that no one was screaming and no one was meditating. The entire monastery was empty. Only the Master was sitting there. This time their curiosity was so great that they entered the monastery and spoke with the Master.

"How is it," they asked, "that some time ago, when we first came upon this monastery, everybody was jumping around and shouting like they were insane? The second time we came, these same people were silently meditating. Now we have returned a third time, and no one is here. Can you explain this to us?"

"It is very simple," said the Master. "When you passed by the first time, the neophytes had just arrived and they were full of the world's madness, so I encouraged them to purge the 10,000 toxins that civilization distributes to everyone. The second time you came, they were exploring the quiet depths of their own innocence, their connections with the universe,

their own human species natures. Now you have come when they have all returned to their homes because they are ready to allow their new consciousness to facilitate the transformation of their communities to more human ways of life. At this moment, I am awaiting the arrival of a new group of neophytes. When you pass by next time, there will again be madness."

THE GREAT INTEGRITY AND OUR ULTIMATE CHOICE

The life style of the Great Integrity, then, is not about withdrawal from civilization, nor about escaping into a life of meditation. It is about engagement with life. It is about commitment to transcending our inhumanity. It is about the process just described.

In other words, the Great Integrity is about a quiet revolution that (1) confronts the pathological yang (purging the old), (2) embraces the yin (entering the temple of our total humanity), and (3) liberates us individually and globally to function through our full species potential (the return of the enlightened ones to the community to be models of personal transformation and agents of social transformation). Lao Tzu's Great Integrity is nothing more nor less than the fulfillment of the potential that was given to us at the evolutionary birth of our species, a condition which took several million years to ripen. How unbelievably privileged we are to be the generations assigned the ultimate task: to be the midwives of our own rebirthing!

How amazing that Lao Tzu, more than two millennia ago, speaks more clearly to us than to his own contemporaries! This unlikely chronological anomaly derives from the historical limitations of Lao Tzu's contemporaries who, at best, could only nod their heads in agreement with Lao Tzu but were able to engage in only the first two aspects of the transcendental process. They were not empowered to be the generations who could facilitate our species rebirth. History has appointed us to this most extraordinary task. If we accept the challenge, and if we are successful, our great great great... grandchildren might live naturally in the Great Integrity that Lao Tzu so clearly foresaw twenty-seven centuries ago.

We are invited to enter the world of Lao Tzu neither as outsiders nor as insiders, neither as activists nor as "passivists", but as more than both. We are the generations of observer-facilitators of our own transformation and the transformation of the premises and institutions of all civilizations from ancient times to the present. These old premises and institutions are now not only contradictions of the Great Integrity, but life threatening to all of us on this planet. Specifically, (1) they have increasingly subverted our very human nature, (2) they have caused thousands of species to become extinct, (3) they have now placed our own species on the endangered list, and (4) they have created the ultimate power to destroy all life on our planet. We haven't much time. Yet, to act in time also requires that we avoid acting untimely. It is not easy.

Who can remain patient
while the mud so gradually clears?
Who can remain still
while the moment for action
so slowly emerges? [16]

We generations of human beings living today may have the awesome ultimate choice between total destruction – what John Somerville called *omnicide* – and total liberation – what Lao Tzu called the *Great Integrity*. We are invited to approach the Great Integrity as peaceful partisans, ready, willing and able to be the "transmogrifiers" for ourselves, for others, and for the planet. It is you and I who will write the final verses of the *Tao Te Ching*. With this

reinvented book as one of our preludes and guides, we begin to prepare ourselves for a New Age of creativity, peace, abundance and planetary synergy.

We are invited to take the first steps in the creation of a world beyond beautiful and ugly, beyond rich and poor, advantaged and disadvantaged, beyond science and religion, labor and profits, intelligent and stupid, left brain and right brain, health and sickness, beyond all the painful dichotomies that civilizations have created.

We know beauty because there is ugly.
We know good because there is evil.
Being and not being,
having and not having,
create each other. [17]

How is it possible to transform our present personal and global malaise into the Great Integrity? There are formidable obstacles:

(1) The extreme fragmentations that define our everyday lives, and that have been inherited for more than two-hundred generations, function as ideological, emotional and experiential entrapments.

(2) The only way of life we know, and that has been known by our parents and by the parents of our parents, expresses the inhumanities and pathologies of a dying social process. We have great difficulty imagining an alternative that has not been widely experienced for thousands of years.

(3) We are programmed by our institutions to accept the miseries of our lives as the only ones possible and desirable. Like the young child who remains dependent and even devoted to the parents who brutalize her (because they are the only parents and the only experience she knows),

we tend to remain loyal to the very political, economic and cultural institutions that threaten our health and our lives.

(4) Living in a world that often robs us of love, respect and beauty, requires escapes that easily become addictive. We are obligingly provided with a great variety: television, films, alcohol, tobacco, various legal and illegal drugs, sexism, racism, male chauvinism, national jingoism, religious sectarianism, addictive foods and drinks, egoism, consumerism, neuroticism, psychoticism, sadism and masochism, just to name a few.

(5) The lack of real political power by the vast majority, compared with the enormous power concentrated in the hands of the economic and political elite, creates the feeling of impotence, which leads to the abdication of political responsibility and the cultivation of cynicism.

But these obstacles are not insurmountable. We have the power to transcend all these entrapments and to acquire a consciousness of the Great Integrity for an alternative way of life. One prerequisite is to be able to step back from our immediate experience and its paralyzing rationalizations.

Lao Tzu's ancient Chinese philosophy provides a window through which we can acquire such a perspective – one that can intellectually catapult us beyond the limitations and toxins of our everyday lives. This window invites us to view the entire evolution of our species in two polarized phases that ancient Chinese philosophy calls *Yin* and *Yang* while the resolution of this polarization clarifies our image of the Great Integrity.

THE EVOLUTION OF CONSCIOUSNESS AS SEEN THROUGH THE METAPHOR OF TWO AND ITS RESOLUTION IN THE GREAT INTEGRITY

To view the entire history of societies and of their corresponding forms of consciousness through the window of two reveals two enormous epochs: 1) the *Yin Epoch*—more than two to five million years of hominid, horde, clan and tribal life characterized for the most part by communal living and expressing a Great Integrity consciousness and a predominance of right cerebral hemispheric intuitive function, and 2) the *Yang Epoch* of the past few thousand years, defined by coercive civilizations, and by the predominance of the left cerebral hemisphere and its hegemony of analytical and alienated consciousness.[18] Lao Tzu in the sixth century BCE and we in the twenty-first century are part of this *Yang Epoch*.

Life today is an expression of the decline and fall of this second great phase, which accounts for the enormous social and individual trauma of our time. Although societies have come and gone in the past, there is a new ultimate danger which the present disintegration of civilization presents: the intolerable juxtaposition of extreme social pathology and high technology, a volatile mixture which can lead not only to the end of civilization, but also to the possibility of our very species extinction. *Speciescide*, and even the possibility of *omnicide*, is avoidable only if we are able to acquire a new consciousness and a third way of life, the very shapes of which were prophetically defined by Lao Tzu. Below is an outline of the two phases, yin and yang, or in Hegel's terms, *thesis* and *antithesis*, along with their future *synthesis* in the third evolutionary phase of the future: integrated planetary community and consciousness, the realization of Lao Tzu's Great Integrity. This third evolutionary phase is now present only embryonically.[19] Its maturation depends upon how we choose to act and to think. Table 2 below views these yin and yang polarized epochs and their resolutions in a future Great Integrity as they are expressed in our principal institutions and cultural modes.

Viewing the entire panorama of human evolution through this widest window of our three mega-epochs reveals the special relevance of Lao Tzu for us today. Epoch I and Epoch III are characterized by the Great Integrity, while Epoch II, the era which began many centuries prior to Lao Tzu and continues to our own time, contradicts the Great Integrity in most every aspect. All of us living today (though we are not all aware of it) are transitional beings struggling (though sometimes counterproductively) to transcend Epoch II — life as fragmentations, sectarianisms and inhumanities — to enter into the Great Harmony of Epoch III.[22]

The transformations of our consciousness, our ways of being, and our institutions require our understanding of and creative participation in this evolutionary process. These transformations demand the emergence of an integral consciousness[23] and the unification of our left and right cerebral hemispheric functions.

What are the transitional forms of this consciousness through which we can begin to step into Epoch III?

(1) The gradual disengagement of our left cerebral cortex from its roles in effectuating and rationalizing our warfare against other human beings, against nature, and against our own essential selves, while further developing the analytical potentialities of this left brain disassociated from its coercive functions.

(2) The increasing engagement of our right cerebral cortex, the part of our consciousness that has been repressed by the hegemony of the left manipulating and rationalizing brain. Fortunately, civilizations have produced compensatory mechanisms, which can function as springboards for facilitating right brain development; for example, the arts, spirituality, "altered" states of consciousness, holistic forms of science and medicine and the cultivation of intuitive and psychic abilities.

(3) Exploring the integration of left brain analysis with right brain intuition to evolve a new meta-scientific consciousness.[23]

(4) Most important of all — the increasing experience of relating to the environment, to each other and to ourselves through the Great Integrity, that is, through a re-humanization, reintegration, and re-harmonization that begins to transcend our Epoch II habits, emotions and institutional forms of fragmentation.

LAO TZU AS THE SILENT PROPHET

Lao Tzu is said to have written the *Tao Te Ching*. However, as we have already pointed out, to have done so would, in itself, be a contradiction to the basic tenets of the book. According to the *Tao Te Ching*, life is to be experienced rather than philosophized.

> *The wise are heard*
> *through their silence,*
> *always self-full through selflessness.*[24]

Sensing this contradiction, one legend tells us that Lao Tzu was never interested in writing out his thoughts, but when he was leaving active life for the seclusion of the wilderness, he was stopped by a gatekeeper at the edge of civilization. This gatekeeper happened to have been one of his disciples. When Lao Tzu tried to pass through the gate, this disciple said to him: "If I let you pass, the world will be forever deprived of your wisdom. I will let you through

	YIN PHASE Tribal Societies Epoch I	YANG PHASE Coercive Civilizations Epoch II	FUTURE Planetary Holism Epoch III
Arts	Magic	Folk, Aesthetic, Commercial Arts	Life as Art
Bodily Movement	Work	Labor, Exercise, Sports, Dance	Integral Movement
Character/Phase	Incipient Phase Birth of Humanity	Caste/Class Phase Technological Revolution	The Great Integrity Rebirth of Humanity
Clothing	Animal skins	Conspicuous Dress	Integral Clothing
Consciousness	Naïve Holism	National, Class, Individual	Human Consciousness
Culture	Clan, Tribal	National, Commercial, Fragmented	Holistic Planetary Culture
Dance	Ceremonial Magic	Formal, Folk, Popular	Improvisation
Economy	Communal	Slavery, Feudalism, Capitalism	Planetary Synergy
Education	Right Brain Magic and Experience	Dominance of Left Brain Reason and rationalization	Left-Right Brain Integral Creativity
Emotions	Functional	Alienated, Schizoid, Compensatory	Unqualified Love
Energy Sources	Sustainable	Coal, Oil, Nuclear Energy, Pollution	Solar, Wind, Water
Food	Gathering, Hunting, Horticulture	Agriculture, Later – Commercial, Artificial Food	Integral Food
Housing	Caves, Tents, Huts	Privatization, Homelessness	Ecological Architecture
Language	Speech	Hierarchal Language Structures	Polystructed Universal "Music" Language
Law	Taboos to preserve integrity of tribe	Laws to Preserve Property Rights	Universal Ethics to Pre- serve the Great Integrity
Music[21]	Ascalar Chanting	Tonal Composition	Polytonal Improvisation
Political Structure	Tribal Democracy	Kingdom, Pseudo-Democracy, Fascism, Bureaucratic Socialism	Planetary Democracy
Recreation	Re-creation of Ability to Renew Life (e.g. Ceremonial Magic)	Compensatory Escapes from Stress	Meta – Re-creation: Exploration of Human Creative Potentials
Relation w/Nature	Unitary	Alienated	Synergistic
Relation w/ Self	Natural Harmony	Schizoid	Integral
Religion	Animism, Magic	Sectarian Religions	Ecumenical Spirituality
Science	Magic	Mechanistic Science	Meta-Science
Social Relations	The Small Harmony Tribal Commune	The Great Fragmentation, Competition, Aggression	The Great Harmony Planetary Community
Therapist	Self, Shaman	Medical Specialist	Preventive Regeneratist Self
Thought	Intuitive	Philosophic	Synergistic
Time Frame	3 + Million Years	Past Five Thousand Years	Future
War	To Defend Living Space	To Establish Hegemony Over Others	Extinct
Work	Socially Necessary Cooperative Life Renewal Activity	Coerced Labor	Creative Fulfillment of Material, Spiritual Needs

only after you write out the principles by which you have led your life." The legend goes on to tell us that Lao Tzu, acceding to the urging and ultimatum of his disciple, wrote the *Tao Te Ching*, and passed through the gate to his reclusive retirement.[25]

But the legend is an unlikely one, even more unlikely than those legends that claim the direct authorship of the books attributed to Sakyamuni, Confucius, Mencius and Chuang Tzu. Contrary to the legend, everything we know about Lao Tzu tells us that he makes no compromises, no bargains with the devil, not even when cajoled by the innocent demands of a well-meaning disciple. Moreover, whereas Confucius, Jesus, Mohammed, Buddha and Moses invite us to be "good" within the framework of an inhuman world, Lao Tzu rejects this world and its premises. He invites us to transcend every false premise of our culture, and to be reborn in the form of our essential humanity, which needs no tests of performance, wealth, achievement or goodness to validate itself. From Lao Tzu's point of view, not even a guidebook is required. The *Tao Te Ching* is more likely to have been the product of many generations of Lao Tzu's disciples.

Lao Tzu is keenly aware that the rules we live by interfere with our essential beingness. He invites us to emancipate ourselves from these rules and suggests that this very act is a key which unlocks the door to our self-realization.

He holds that we are deserving regardless of our achievements or contributions. We deserve to fulfill our material and our spiritual needs simply because we are human beings, and certainly not because we fulfill the conditionalities that our manipulative institutions demand. Twenty-seven centuries later, we are at last pregnant with a post-civilized world modeled after Lao Tzu's main premises. Indeed, he was certainly an extraordinarily prophetic wise man.

The Great Integrity is love. It is the love that uniquely expresses our deepest unarmored bonds with each other. On the highest level we become love. Our language, like all other aspects of our culture, tends to obfuscate our loss of wholeness and humanity. Since the experience of love requires this very wholeness and humanity that we have for the most part lost, our use of the term most often refers to the perversions of love that are compensatory for this loss. We might differentiate five types of love. The first three are pathological contradictions of the Great Integrity, and the last two are healthy expressions of it.

The first type is *possessive love*, that is loving an object because we are capable of possessing it, or at least believing that we possess it. Even one's mate might be loved as an object. This is the most alienated form of love and is widely practiced since the civilizations of the past five thousand years have been focused on possessing. All objects are viewed for their value to exchange and accumulate. Success is defined as the power to accrue and maintain the largest number of desirable objects. People too are objectified, primarily as the means to create the objects to be acquired, so control over those who produce those objects becomes a basic test of success. The objectification of nature and of human labor, when extended to personal relations takes many forms, for example, male chauvinism, which is a typical expression of love as possession. Clearly, objective love is not only toxic to our humanity, but inverts and perverts the very act of loving itself, turning it from a selfless and spontaneous experience of human fulfillment to a selfish and manipulative act.

The second type of love is sometimes referred to as *codependent love*. It is rooted in the experience of powerlessness and expresses itself as an addiction to control or to be controlled. A relationship of codependent love is a struggle for competing dependencies and results in the mutual exploitation of immaturities. Codependency prevents self-growth and independence, as well as genuine fulfillments. It is also a contradiction of the Great Integrity, but on a lesser level than the first possessive type of love.

The third type of love might be called *romantic love*. It is generally an unconscious escapist attempt to compensate for the absence of self-appreciation. It is therefore generally a search for that "perfect" mate who is imagined as having the qualities that the romantic lover lacks. Although less pathological than possessive or codependent love, romantic love also contradicts the Great Integrity by its compensatory functions that drive a wedge between the essential self and the imagined deficient self, as well as between the essential other and the imagined "perfect" mate.

The fourth type of love is *subjective love*. It is the expression of a state of lovingness. There are no ulterior motives, no objects of material value to be acquired. The person who experiences subjective love is relatively without armor. Love is freely given and received. In such love, we are not fixated on a single possessive or codependent or romantic object of our love, but we love, and are loved by many people. Moreover, in subjective love, not only human beings, but animals, birds, plants, rocks, art, the entire gamut of nature and of the environment, the entire universe tends to be experienced in a loving way. In this fourth form of love, many layers of armoring are shed, and we live more in harmony with each other, with nature and with our own human natures. It is the healthiest and most fulfilling level of love that our present epoch of transition offers as a potential expression of the Great Integrity.

In the fifth type, we will experience love beyond its objective and subjective forms. We will *become love*. It is the experience of our total humanity, stripped of every shred of alienation, stripped of every premise of aggressive civilization. It is complete self and social actualization. Indeed, it is the ideal state of being that Lao Tzu defines as the Great Integrity, and is realizable only in the Third Epoch.[26]

As long as we live within acquisitive societies, we will be deprived of the fifth type of love, which is to say that all of us today are incapable of fully experiencing the Great Integrity. Within civilization, the Great Integrity can only be dreamed, sensed, and vicariously or tentatively experienced. It cannot define the everyday experiential core of our being until we live an alternative life style that has completely healed the divisions between privileged and underprivileged, left and right brain, between us and them, and between the ego us and the id us. The Great Integrity requires the transcendence of all the fragmentations that have defined our personal and social lives during the past few millennia. Lao Tzu's Great Integrity is nothing less than the total liberation of each and all of us to experience this universe in its own terms, transcending all objectivities and subjectivities while never having to sacrifice our humanity, that is, our ability to function with a higher consciousness than the rest of nature.

Such a state is difficult for us to imagine since it lies so beyond the capabilities of our everyday experience which is still locked in the chains of civilization. At this point in time, Lao Tzu's *Guide to the Theory and Practice of the Great Integrity* allows us a closer look at our future, a clearer glimpse of its shapes and feelings, and an insight into our own uncorrupted Essence that is reborn on a higher level each moment that we take another step toward our own emancipation.

Preface

This is to share with the reader why and how I wrote this translation and commentary on Lao Tzu's *Tao Te Ching*.[1]

WHY I WROTE THIS BOOK

Lao Tzu, the legendary wise man of the sixth century BCE was a rebel. We can summarize his point of view in five main premises:

(1) It is the origin and nature of the universe to be integral, that is, for the whole to be contained in every part and for every part to be inextricable from the whole.[2] Lao Tzu referred to this characterization of reality as the Tao,[3] that is, the Great Integrity. Everything and every living organism expresses itself as part of this Great Integrity.[4]

(2) In what Lao Tzu called "ancient times"[5], human beings, just as every other species, also lived in harmony with the Great Integrity.[6]

(3) However, all this changed for us human beings living in relatively recent "civilized" times when we became separated from nature and began relating to our environment, to each other, and even to ourselves, as enemies to be conquered. Lao Tzu attributes this disassociation[7] to the loss of the Great Integrity. He concludes that it is this loss which is the root of all the forms of misery that human beings experience — inequities, injustices, coercion, manipulation, selfishness, decadence, crime, war, and all the various types of falsifications, addictions and corruptions that pervade our lives.[8]

(4) Some day we will all return to the Great Integrity as the form and substance of all our lives.[9]

(5) The Great Integrity is not only an alternative way of life that we can realize some time in the future, but it is the very pathway to our transcendence. The implication is that the Great Integrity is a guide for our behavior and consciousness right now as we reinvent our institutions and ourselves.

I believe that I, and many of my contemporaries, relate to these propositions, even more enthusiastically than Lao Tzu's contemporaries did. Indeed, this is my primary motivation to translate and apply Lao Tzu's thinking directly to our own lives today. Specifically, I can think of four main reasons why so many of us nowadays are even more in tune with Lao Tzu's ideas than were the people of his own time:

(1) Our modern experience of violating the Great Integrity has not diminished since Lao Tzu's time, but has in many ways escalated. For example, we have learned to murder each other more efficiently and in geometrically much larger numbers than people were capable of during any previous era. This is one of several new conditions of life today that differentiates our choices from those of Lao Tzu's contemporaries. In the sixth century BCE, if the Great Integrity

were not recovered, life would, and in fact did, go on. In the twenty-first century if we fail to recover the Great Integrity, we are likely to bring about our own species extinction.

(2) Modern physics (relativity theory and quantum mechanics) as well as other new research (that will be briefly discussed below in this Preface), has provided a scientific basis for Lao Tzu's theory of the Great Integrity.

(3) Many modern studies in anthropology, sociology, history, psychology and philosophy have corroborated Lao Tzu's contention that human beings are not born inhuman, but have been trained to be so only in more recent times.[10] Therefore, we now know that the Great Integrity is more in harmony with human nature than with the greed and coercion that is almost universally practiced.[11]

(4) Our new technologies have such an incredible potential that it is now possible to produce a planetary abundance for a healthy life for human beings everywhere.[12] Indeed, we have achieved the global material and communication bases for reestablishing Lao Tzu's Great Integrity. Recent studies have provided insights that these transformations in life and consciousness are already well under way.[13]

However, my unconscious identification with Lao Tzu and the Great Integrity long preceded my introduction to this great wise man. Like Lao Tzu, I am a rebel. Even in my childhood, I rebelled against "schooling". Ever since I was in the fourth grade in elementary school, it was rare for me to arrive on time. School started at 9 AM. I would usually get there one or two hours late each day. Having missed the school bus, I would either walk the two or three miles or hitchhike. I hardly ever did any homework unless threatened by a teacher with dire consequences. Most of the time I lived in my own world, and only paid

sufficient attention to receive high marks in my examinations. Junior and Senior High School were very much the same. This rebelliousness against "schooling" began almost half a century before I read:

Schooling stuffs the brains of our children with trivia.
The more the trivia, the more their anxieties.
They indoctrinate the children to believe that the
consequences are grave when they fail to
distinguish "good" from "evil",
and agreement from disagreement.
What gross nonsense![14]

I remember only one lesson in all my years of elementary school that reached me. I was ten years old, in the fifth grade, and my teacher, Miss Kilgallen, was at the blackboard introducing us to the idea that sentences had a structure. She wrote the subject and verb of a sentence and then drew diagonal lines from these two hegemonic entities indicating how all other words in the sentence were modifiers and dependents of these two fundamental entities. I lit up like a Christmas tree! Language had structure! Maybe everything and everybody in the world has structure and we are all related! Maybe I could understand and become part of all these relationships! Maybe my life has meaning and I could understand its meaning!

How fantastic! It was a day that changed my life, and so began my unconscious search for Lao Tzu who was not introduced to me until 1977 when I was fifty-six years old. In-between my tenth and fifty-sixth years, there were some landmark experiences that drew me closer to my sixth century BCE soul brother.

My first college degree was in geography and photogrammetry (making maps from aerial photographs). In 1943, I went directly from college into the armed services and during World War II, I was in charge of photogrammetry for the U.S. Navy in the Pacific Command. My last assignment of the war was to make the photomaps of the landing beaches that guided U.S. troops in the invasion of Japan. Because of my position at the Joint Intelligence Center in Pearl Harbor, I became intimately aware of the atrocities committed by the Japanese, and was one of the first to observe the photographs of the unbelievable devastation caused by the Hiroshima and Nagasaki atomic bombs. These experiences were critical in my decision to devote my life to exploring how we came to lose our humanity and our connections to what I believed to be an inherently friendly and interconnected universe, and how we might regain these connections and recover our humanity. Although I hadn't yet heard about the Great Integrity, my intuition and my growing intellectual understanding convinced me of the interconnectiveness of all entities, and that it was possible to create a more human social condition than the one into which I was born.

I couldn't visualize how making maps from aerial photographs could take me down this path in any significant way, so I decided to prepare myself for a different profession. It seemed to me that music had the harmony and integrity I longed for and that I could compose and perform music to help awaken people to the possibilities of living in a higher state of consciousness and humanity. Thirty years before I "met" Lao Tzu, my goals in life were to be among those –

> who nourish our community with a
> benevolent heart as deep as an abyss,
> who are incapable of lies and injustices,
> and whose natural rhythms of action play midwife
> to the highest good of each pregnant moment. [15]

So I went to the Juilliard School of Music and became a composer, conductor, musicologist and teacher. I taught at Brooklyn and Queens Colleges in New York City and became the chairman of the music departments at C.W. Post

College of Long Island University, Fairleigh Dickinson University and of the Integrated Arts Department at Hunter College High School.

It was during my twenty-five year romance with music, poetry, and all the arts that I became convinced that because we human beings violate our own humanity and the innate integrity of the universe, we are compelled to seek out religious and artistic experience as compensations for the fragmentations and other distortions we create in our lives. I tried to make the kind of music that might help to stimulate an alternative consciousness and way of being that was more like music. I was in constant search for the Great Integrity, before I ever knew the word *Tao*. This was my unconscious quarter of a century apprenticeship for translating Lao Tzu's five thousand-character song of the Tao into a hymn to our own hearts and dreams.

But there was another thirty-year apprenticeship that took me into the world of Lao Tzu even more directly – through Chinese medicine and philosophy.

It all began in a physician's office when in the process of utilizing a metal syringe, he accidentally jammed the instrument through my auricular tympanic membrane, through the middle ear, and injuring the organ of Corti in the inner ear. The resulting condition, known as Meniere's Syndrome is a combination of deafness, vertigo and tinnitus (ringing in the ear). I consulted with six otologists, all of whom had the same mantra: "Meniere's is incurable, and it isn't the worst disease you could have." I couldn't think of anything worse – especially for a musician. Being a very stubborn and persistent person, and knowing that what conventional medicine means when they say that a disease is incurable is that they don't have a drug or a surgical procedure for that particular problem, I decided I was going to have to find my own cure.

I began with a strict therapeutic nutritional regime that I learned from the Japanese traditional physician, Dr. George Ohsawa in 1960, on his first trip to the U.S., about ten years before this accident. Dr. Ohsawa developed the nutritional theory and practice that he called *macrobiotics*, from the principles of oriental medicine. Although he was a master acupuncture physician, he hardly ever treated a patient since he was very clear that his mission in life was to teach people throughout the world how to prevent and cure their own illnesses by taking responsibility for their nutrition and life styles. However, macrobiotics did not cure my Meniere's.

I had become a friend of Dr. Ohsawa during his subsequent frequent trips to the U.S., and therefore had the opportunity to observe him on two very rare occasions when he treated two medical doctors with acupuncture. I was very impressed with the quick results he achieved, but at that time I was not motivated to learn acupuncture, nor was George motivated to teach it. However, in 1972 when macrobiotics failed to cure my Meniere's I thought that acupuncture might, and I searched for someone who could teach me. At that time, very few people even knew what acupuncture was, and to find an expert in the U.S. was not likely. However, Carl Jung's principle that there are no accidents, only synchronicities, was at work. I was living at that time in Florida, and voilà! – I was introduced to a young man, Dr. Cheng Wai-Fung, who had just completed his acupuncture studies in Hong Kong!

I told him that I was going to be his first student. "In no way would that be possible", he said. "There are no manuals in English and I've never taught anyone anything in my life. It will just not work!" But my need was great and so was my persistence. After that accident, I became very wary of the dangers of the doctor-patient relationship. From then on, I was going to rely

primarily on myself for the prevention and treatment of illness. I refused to accept his refusal to teach me. Eventually, we sat down and, over time, he translated his manual for me, point-by-point, meridian-by-meridian, principle by principle.

When I thought I knew enough to begin to treat my Meniere's Syndrome, I started to needle myself every day, then every other day. In two months I cured my "incurable disease"! I was amazed and so grateful that I decided to devote the next segment of my life to acupuncture and the study of the principles of oriental medicine and philosophy. I went to Japan and Taiwan and studied with masters there.

Upon my return to the U.S., I began a clinical practice, researching and teaching. Since there were no practical materials in English, I also began to write and publish books, articles, charts, videotapes and audiotapes, at first, primarily for my students. During my thirty years of devotion to acupuncture and alternative medicine, I became one of the leading authorities, having written more than seventy publications. I began to teach seminars for physicians whose interest in learning acupuncture was first stimulated by President Nixon's initial visit to China in 1972. Later I joined the adjunct faculties of several chiropractic colleges that began to offer acupuncture in continuing education programs, and I designed and taught the acupuncture continuing medical education curriculum for the University of Miami School of Medicine. The development and teaching of these programs facilitated my reconciling oriental medicine and philosophy with the premises and problems of modern medicine and science. I became more aware of how the evolution of eastern and western civilizations and their divergent ways of thinking could be integrated to provide alternatives to the personal, social and institutional crises that now challenge our well being and our very lives.

In my research, one of the earliest discoveries I made was the theory and clinical applications of what I called *micro-acupuncture*, specifically showing that thirty parts of the body[16] function as bioenergetic systems that have the potential to diagnose and to treat the entire body,[17] and that the topologies of the micro-acupoints are holonomic reiterations of the anatomy.[18] In three of these micro-systems it has been shown that there are micro-acupuncture meridians (channels) of bioenergetics (Qi) that holonomically reiterate the topological pathways of the fourteen main channels of traditional Chinese acupuncture.[19] These discoveries provide scientific evidence for Lao Tzu's intuitive concept of the Tao, which characterizes the universe as an indivisible unity in which every part is inextricable from the whole and the whole is inextricable from every part.[20]

In the theory of micro-acupuncture, although only thirty parts of the body are shown to be microcosms of the macro-energetics and anatomy, the implication of this research is that every part of every organism expresses the whole right down to the cellular and micro-particle levels.[21] Recent microbiology research supports this premise.[22] The scientific bases of Lao Tzu's Great Integrity are also validated by neurophysiologists[23] and by physicists.[24]

My first introduction to the *Tao Te Ching* was through a gift of the Gia-Fu Feng and Jane English translation that I received from a dear friend, Sarena Morello, in June 1977. I had already published several articles on my discoveries of micro-acupuncture, and I knew, as soon as I began reading the book, that Lao Tzu had been a long unconscious spiritual comrade who was to become a very important and conscious part of my life and thought.

HOW I WROTE THIS BOOK.

My Chinese is much too rudimentary to have directly translated the *Tao Te Ching* from Chinese to English. I mainly relied upon two different manuscripts that provided translations of the multiple English equivalents of each Chinese character of the eighty-one sections. One manuscript was written for me by Professor Yan Cheng[25] who assisted me for twelve years, researching publications written only in Chinese, providing English-Chinese and Chinese-English translations, and computerizing my manuscripts in preparation for publication. The other translation was written by Chi Choo-Li in collaboration with my friend, Mark Johnson,[26] one of the leading authorities in the U.S. on Qi Gong, Feng Shui and ancient Chinese philosophy. Also useful was the Chinese-English character-by-character translation by Gregory C. Richter, although this book provides only one English meaning for each Chinese character.[27] Lastly, I was fortunate to have discovered Jonathan Star's scholarly work before completing my manuscript. Star lists the multiple possible meanings of each character.[28] I was also grateful for the twenty-eight English translations of the *Tao Te Ching* that are part of my own personal library.[29]

My criteria in the translations were:
(1) To render the most poetic translations in English that I could. Although the original Chinese is written more as prose than poetry, I felt that the central ideas, being more paradoxical than logical, demanded a language that transcended language, and that task fundamentally requires poetry.

(2) To create a consistency and integrity for each of the eighty-one verses. Although the original manuscript consisted of a single five thousand-character document, almost all translators have accepted the later eighty-one section divisions. I felt that this division is useful and practical,

offering the reader a potential special meditative focus for each section. I have supported this eighty-one part division in three main ways: 1) By shaping a thematic constancy within each verse, 2) By giving a title to each verse that identifies its particular focus, and 3) By allowing the last stanza to serve as a summary of the main implications of the verse.

To make a language bridge between Lao Tzu's intent and its specific meanings for us today.

My criteria for the commentaries were:
(1) To define the principle focus for each verse.

(2) To translate this focus in terms of its relevancy for us today.

(3) To show both the personal and social implications of each verse for the transformations in our consciousness, life styles and institutions that are sometimes consciously, sometimes unconsciously on our current wish lists.

(4) To provide a scientific basis for, as well as an intuitive harmony with, Lao Tzu's Great Integrity.

All of the above is to say that, because in the Great Integrity we are all inseparable, in the following pages, I invite you as a friend to join me in an amazing adventure that allows us to tune into Lao Tzu's wisdom of two and a half millennia ago as a song that he is singing to each and all of us, as though he were living in our own hearts, dreams and alternatives.

Ralph Alan Dale
June 2002

Tao Te Ching

THE VERSES

老子
道可道非常道名可名非常名無名天地之始
有名萬物之母常無欲以觀其妙常有欲以觀
其徼此兩者同出而異名同謂之玄玄之又玄眾
妙之門

The Tao that can be told
is not the universal Tao.
The name that can be named
is not the universal name.

In the infancy of the universe,
there were no names.
Naming fragments the mysteries of life
into ten thousand things and their manifestations.

Yet mysteries and manifestations
spring from the same source:
The Great Integrity
which is the mystery within manifestation,
the manifestation within mystery,
the naming of the unnamed,
and the un-naming of the named.

When these interpenetrations
are in full attendance,
we will pass the gates of naming notions
in our journey toward transcendence.

2 RELATIVITY

天下皆知美之為美斯惡已皆知善之為善斯不
善已故有無之相生難易之相成長短之相形高
下之相傾音聲之相和前後之相隨是以聖人處
無為之事行不言之教萬物作而不辭生而不
有為而不恃功成不居夫唯不居是以不去

We know beauty because there is ugly.
We know good because there is evil.
Being and not being,
having and not having,
create each other.

Difficult and easy,
long and short,
high and low,
define each other,
just as before and after follow each other.

The dialectic of sound gives voice to music,
always transforming "is" from "was"
as the ancestors of "to be".

The wise
teach without telling,
allow without commanding,
have without possessing,
care without claiming.

In this way we harvest eternal importance
because we never announce it.

道德經 5

不尚賢使民不爭不貴難得之貨使民不為
盜不見可欲使心不亂是以聖人之治也虛其心實
其腹弱其志強其骨常使民無知無欲使夫知
者不敢為也為無為則無不治矣
。

Overpraising the gifted leads to contentiousness.
Overvaluing the precious invites stealing.
Craving the desirable loses contentment.

The natural person
desires without craving
and acts without excess.

By not doing,
everything is done.

道德經 7

道沖而用之或不盈淵乎似萬物之宗挫其銳
解其紛和其光同其塵湛兮似若存吾不知
其誰之子象帝之先

The Great Integrity is an endless abyss,
Yet, it is the inexhaustibly fertile
source of the universe.

It blunts all sharpness,
unties the entangled,
and merges with the dust!

Hidden but ever present—
this parent of the gods—
whose child may it be?

天地不仁以萬物為芻狗聖人不仁以百姓為芻
天地之間其猶橐籥乎虛而不屈動而愈
出多言數窮不如守中

Yin and yang aren't sentimental.
They exist without moralizing.
They act regardless of our wishes
within the ebb and flow
of every pregnant moment.

The space between yin and yang
is like a bellows –
empty, yet infinitely full.
The more it yields,
the more it fills.

Countless words
count less
than the silent balance
between yin and yang.

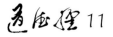

6 LIFE'S SPIRIT

谷神不死是謂玄牝玄牝之門是謂天地根
綿綿若存用之不勤

The spirit of life
never dies.

It is the infinite gateway
to mysteries within mysteries.

It is the seed of yin,
the spark of yang.

Always elusive,
endlessly available.

13

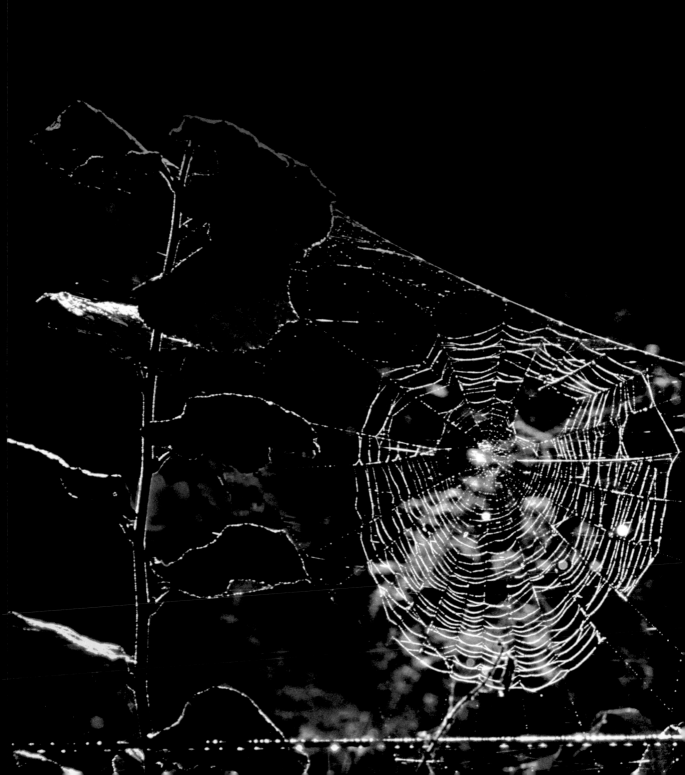

Verse 7 MODESTY

The Great Integrity, having had no birth,
expresses its immortality
without pronouncements.

The wise are heard
through their silence,
always self-full through selflessness.

天長地久天地所以能長且久者以其不自生故

能長生是以聖人後其身而身先外其身而身

存非以其無私耶故能成其私

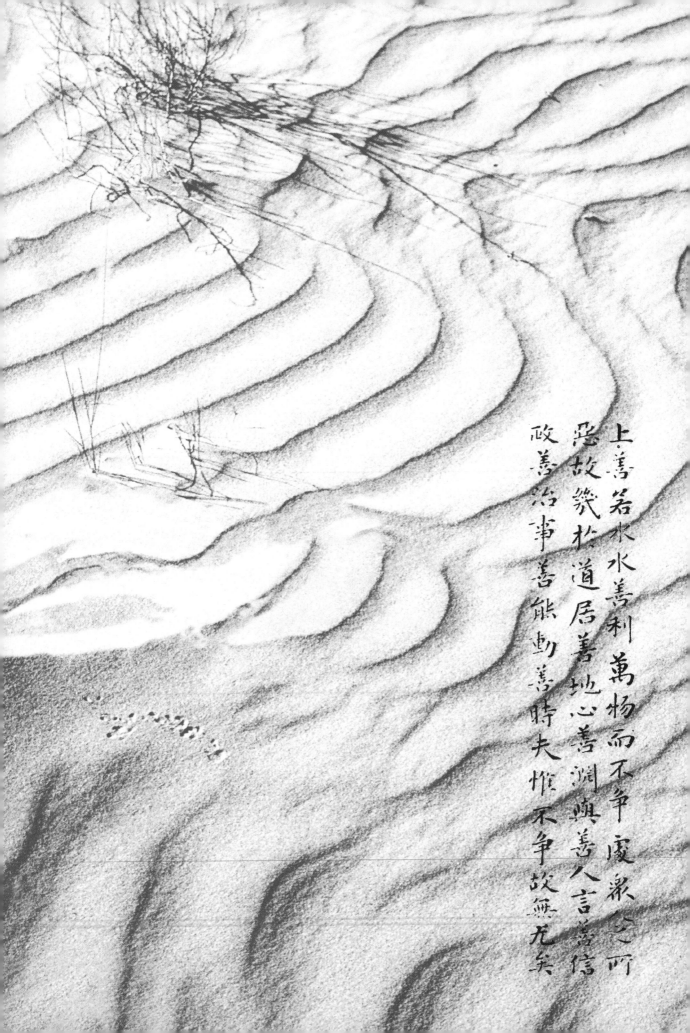

上善若水水善利萬物而不爭處眾人之所
惡故幾於道居善地心善淵與善人言善信
政善治事善能動善時夫惟不爭故無尤矣

Verse 8 THE HIGHEST GOOD

The highest good is like water,
nourishing life effortlessly,
flowing without prejudice
to the lowliest places.

It springs from all
who nourish their community
with a benevolent heart as deep as an abyss,
who are incapable of lies and injustices,
who are rooted in the earth,
and whose natural rhythms of action
play midwife to the highest good
of each pregnant moment.

Keep filling your bowl,
and it will spill over.

Keep sharpening your knife,
and it will blunt.

Keep hoarding gold in your house,
and you will be robbed.

Keep seeking approval,
and you will be chained.

The Great Integrity leads to actualization,
never overfulfillment.

持而盈之不如其已揣而銳不可長保金玉滿
堂莫之能守富貴而驕自遺其咎功成名遂
身退天之道

道德經 19

載營魄抱一能無離乎專氣致柔能如嬰兒
乎滌除玄覽能無疵乎愛民治國能無為乎
天門開闔能無雌乎明白四達能無知乎生之
畜之生而不有為而不恃長而不宰是謂玄德

10 LIMITATIONS

When embracing the unity
of mind, body, emotions and spiritual being,
can we transcend our fragmentations
without leaving a trace?

When Qi Gong sculpts sinew suppleness,
can our flesh become soft as a new born babe?

Can we cleanse the inner vision,
leaving mind in spiritual purity?

Can our affairs of the heart,
and our affairs of state
be so unconditional
that we grant unqualified permissibility?

Can the gate to Yin be opened
without inviting Yang?

Can our reasoning mind be purged of coercion,
allowing our heart its unfettered joy?

Can we act like every other species,
seeking no reward,
taking no pride,
guiding without enslaving?

Such is our vision of the Great Integrity
on whose path we have at last planted both feet,
ready to move, step by step,
until we arrive at the great unfettered gate.

三十輻共一轂當其無有車之用埏埴以為器
當其無有器之用鑿戶牖以為室當其無有
室之用故有之以為利無之以為用

*We join thirty spokes
to the hub of a wheel,
yet it's the center hole
that drives the chariot.*

*We shape clay
to birth a vessel,
yet it's the hollow within
that makes it useful.*

*We chisel doors and windows
to construct a room,
yet it's the inner space
that makes it livable.*

*Thus do we
create what is
to use what is not.*

道德經 23

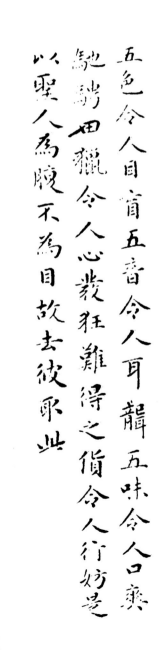

五色令人目盲五音令人耳聾 五味令人口爽
馳騁田獵 令人心發狂 難得之貨令人行妨是
以聖人為腹 不為目 故去彼取此

Colors can make us blind!
Music can make us deaf!
Flavors can destroy our taste!
Possessions can close our options!
Racing can drive us mad
and its rewards obstruct our peace!

Thus, the wise
fill the inner gut
rather than the eyes,
always sacrificing the superficial
for the essential.

25

13 IDENTITY

Accolades can usher in
great trouble for your body.
Censure can herald misery.

Why can favor and disfavor
both be harmful?

Because both accolades and censure,
when filtered through self as ego,
always place us in jeopardy.

But when the universe becomes your self,
when you love the world as yourself,
all reality becomes your haven,
reinventing you as your own heaven.

Only then, will you transcend tense
to fully be here now.
Only then, no harm
will the universe proffer
nor you to her,
for you will be
not you but she
and both–the universal Great Integrity.

寵辱若驚貴大患若身何謂辱寵為下得
之若驚失之若驚是謂寵辱若驚何謂貴大
患若身吾所以有大患者為吾有身及吾無身
吾有何患故貴以身為天下若可寄天下愛以
身為天下若可託天下

視之不見名曰夷聽之不聞名曰希搏之不得
名曰微此三者不可致詰故混而為一其上不
皦其下不昧繩繩兮不可名復歸於無物是謂
無狀之狀無物之象是謂惚恍迎之不見其
首隨之不見其後執古之道以御今之有能知
古始是謂道紀

Verse 14 BEYOND REASON

That which we look at
but cannot see is the invisible.

That which we listen to
but cannot hear is the inaudible.

That which we reach for
but cannot grasp is the intangible.

Beyond reason, these three merge,
contradicting experience.

Their rising side isn't bright.
Their setting side isn't dark.

Sense-less, unnamable, they return
to the realms of nothingness.

Form without form,
image without image,
indefinable, ineluctable, elusive.

Confronting them, you see no beginning.
Following them, you see no end.

Yet, riding the plowless plow
can seed the timeless Tao,
harvesting the secret
transcendence of the Now.

In ancient times
the people knew the Great Integrity
with subtlety and profundity.

Because they are so unfathomable to us,
we can describe the ancients
only with great effort.

They were–
cautious as those crossing an icy stream,
wary as those surrounded by dangers,
dignified as guests,
yielding as melting ice,
innocent as virgin wood,
open and broad as valleys,
merging freely as muddy water.

But today, who can remain patient
while the mud so gradually clears?
Who can remain still
while the moment for action
so slowly emerges?

Who?
We observers of the Great Integrity,
who in our times,
like those ancients,
never seeking fulfillment,
are never unfulfilled.

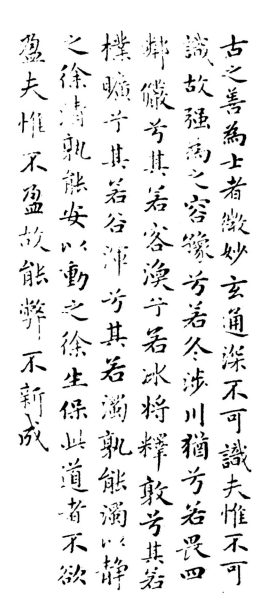

Verse
16 TRANQUILLITY

Allow the heart to empty itself of all turmoil!
Retrieve the utter tranquillity of mind
from which you issued.

Although all forms are dynamic,
and we all grow and transform,
each of us is compelled to return to our root.
Our root is quietude.

To fully return to our root is to be enlightened.
Never to experience tranquillity is to act blindly,
a sure path to disaster.

To know tranquillity is to embrace all.
To embrace all is to be just.
Justice is the foundation for wholeness.
Wholeness is the Great Integrity.
The Great Integrity is the infinite fulfilling itself.

33

太上下知有之其次親之譽之其次畏之侮之故
信不足焉有不信猶兮其貴言功成事遂百
姓皆謂我自然

There are four types of leaders:
The best leader is indistinguishable
from the will of those who selected her.
The next best leader enjoys the love
and praise of the people.
The poor leader rules through coercion and fear.
And the worst leader is a tyrant despised
by the multitudes who are the victims of his power.

What a world of difference among these leaders!
In the last two types, what is done
is without sincerity or trust—only coercion.
In the second type, there is a harmony
between the leader and the people.
In the first type, whatever is done happens
so naturally that no one presumes to take the credit!

大道癈有仁義智惠出有大偽六親不和有孝慈國家昏亂有忠臣

18 THE PARADOXES OF ABANDONING THE GREAT INTEGRITY

When the Great Integrity was abandoned,
humanity and justice appeared.

When knowledge and teachers appeared,
hypocrisy was their inevitable accompaniment.

When family relationships lost their harmony,
filial piety and parental affection were suddenly birthed.

When a nation succumbs to chaos and corruption,
patriotic politicians are always at hand announcing themselves.

絶
聖
棄
智
民
利
百
倍
絶
仁
棄
義
民
復
孝
慈

絶
巧
棄
利
盜
賊
無
有
此
三
者
以
為
文
不
足
故

令
有
所
屬
見
素
抱
樸
少
私
寡
欲

Banish the intellectual!
Discard knowledge!
We will all benefit a hundredfold!

Eliminate all institutions of charity and justice!
We can then return
to our natural love for each other.

Let everyone be released
from our addictions to shrewdness and profit!
Then, thievery will disappear!

These three negate the Great Integrity.
But to negate these negations is insufficient.
Three affirmations are also necessary.

The first is to embrace simplicity and integrity.
The second is to consume only the needs of our body and soul.
The third is to allow our love and concern for others to define our essentiality.

絕學無憂唯之與阿相去幾何善之與惡相
去何若人之所畏不可不畏荒兮其未央眾
人熙熙如享太牢如登春臺我獨泊兮其未兆
若嬰兒之未孩乘乘兮若無所歸眾人皆有
餘我獨若遺我愚人之心也哉沌沌兮俗人昭
昭我獨若昏俗人察察我獨悶悶澹兮其
若海飂兮似無所止眾人皆有以我獨頑似鄙
我獨異於人而貴求食於母

20 THE SADNESS OF SUPERFICIALITIES AND OF THE UNFULFILLED GREAT INTEGRITY

It is sometimes deeply depressing to be a rebel,
knowing that we can never share most people's way of life, nor can they share ours.

Schooling stuffs the brains of our children with trivia.
The more the trivia, the more their anxieties.
They indoctrinate the children to believe that the consequences are grave
when they fail to distinguish "good" from "evil", and agreement from disagreement.
What gross nonsense!

To escape the rubbish of all this so-called knowledge,
in the winter people run to the great feasts of lamb, pork and ox,
and they climb high in the mountains to view the first signs of spring.

We are so different! Having no desire for the trivialities,
nor for their compensations, we are like infants not yet knowing how to laugh!
Ever wandering, and having no home to which we may return.

While most people are obsessed with superficialities, we feel empty.
While most people feel they know so much, we feel simple-minded.
While most people believe they live happily in the best of all possible worlds,
we are despaired to witness this world!
It is so painful to know that we will always be outsiders,
endlessly moving like the ocean, aimlessly blowing like the wind.

While we fear what others fear, we don't treasure what others treasure.
Our treasure is the Great Integrity.
However, until it is shared, it will not be the Universal Integrity,
for we are part of them, and they are part of us.

21

THE GREAT INTEGRITY IS A PARADOX

孔德之容惟道是從道之為物惟恍惟惚
惚兮恍兮其中有象恍兮惚兮其中有物窈兮
冥兮其中有精其精甚真其中有信自古
及今其名不去以閱眾甫吾何以知眾甫之
然哉以此

The Great Integrity is a paradox.
It is inherent in the universe,
yet its form is so illusive.
It is the Vital Essence of every entity,
yet nothing announces its essential character.

The Great Integrity was apparent
before time, space and matter appeared to separate.
How can we re-mind and re-infuse ourselves
with this very touchstone of all essentialities and connections?

By re-fusing time, space and matter
with the spiritualization of our materiality,
and with the materialization of our spirituality.

Then, when our dualities and numeralities
become blurred and forgotten,
the Great Integrity will re-emerge in forms
of such incredible depths and dimensions of enlightenment,
precisely because our temporary fragmentary consciousness
created a multi-millennial amnesia.

Verse
22 CELEBRATE PARADOX!

曲則全枉則直窪則盈弊則新少則得多
則惑是以聖人抱一為天下式不自見故明不
自是故彰不自伐故有功不自矜故長夫惟
不爭故天下莫能與之爭古之所謂曲則全
者豈虛言哉故誠全而歸之

No-thing remains itself.
Each prepares the path to its opposite.

To be ready for wholeness, first be fragmented.
To be ready for rightness, first be wronged.
To be ready for fullness, first be empty.
To be ready for renewal, first be worn out.
To be ready for success, first fail.
To be ready for doubt, first be certain.

Because the wise observe the world
through the Great Integrity,
they know they are not knowledgeable.
Because they do not perceive
only through their perceptions,
they do not judge this right and that wrong.
Because they do not delight in boasting,
they are appreciated.
Because they do not announce their superiority,
they are acclaimed.
Because they never compete,
no one can compete with them.

Verily, fragmentation prepares the path to wholeness,
the mother of all origins and realizations.

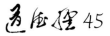 45

希言自然飄風不終朝驟雨不終日孰為此
者天地天地尚不能久而況於人乎故從事
於道者道者同於道德者同於德失者同
於失同於道者道亦得之同於德者德亦得
之同於失者失亦得之信不足焉有不信焉
政者不立跨者不行自見者不明自是者不
彰自伐者無功自矜者不長其於道也曰餘
食贅行物或惡之故有道者不處也

23 SINCERITY

Speak few words, but say them with quietude and sincerity,
and they will be long lasting,
for a raging wind cannot blow all morning,
nor a sudden rainstorm last throughout the day.

Why is this so?
Because it is the nature of the sky and the earth to be frugal.
Even human beings cannot alter this nature
without suffering the consequences.

When we sincerely follow the ethical path,
we become one with it.
When we become one with the ethical path, it embraces us.

When we completely lose our way, we become one with loss.
When we become one with loss, loss embraces us.

When we sincerely follow the Great Integrity,
we become one with it.
When we are one with the Great Integrity, it embraces us.

But when nothing is done sincerely,
no-thing and no one embraces us.

Verse
24 AVOIDING VOIDS

食贅行物或惡之故有道者不處也
彰自伐者無功自矜者不長其於道也曰餘
政者不立跨者不行自見者不明自是者不

Standing on tiptoe will only make you tipsy,
Walking with long strides will not allow a long walk.
Shining the light on yourself will never enlighten you.
Being self-righteous precludes you from being right.
Boasting about yourself will never boost your eminence.
Parading yourself parodies leadership.

Tao consciousness avoids
the cultivation of all these ego bloated voids.

道德經 49

有物混成先天地生寂兮寥兮獨立而不改
周行而不殆可以為天下母吾不知其名
字之名曰大大曰逝逝曰遠遠曰返故
道大天大地大王亦大域中有四大而王居
其一焉人法地地法天天法道道法自然

Verse 25 NAMING THE NAMELESS

What preceded life? The earth.
What preceded the earth? The universe.
What preceded the universe?
The soundless and shapeless, origin of origins,
ever transforming and having no beginning nor end.

This Mother of the universe is boundless, and nameless.
But if we wanted to share with you anything
about this remarkable non-executing executor,
we must invent a name for it.

We will call it the Tao because Tao means great.
Incredibly great because it occupies infinite space,
being fully present in the whole universe, and in every infinitesimal particle.

Because this Great Integrity created the universe,
and the universe created the earth,
and the earth created us, we are all incredibly great.

Life derives from the nature of the earth.
The earth derives from the nature of the universe.
The universe derives from the nature of the Great Integrity.
And the Great Integrity is the omnipresent, omnigenous omniform,
the universal material and spiritual substance,
and the holoversal interlinkage and coition of existence.

重為輕根靜為躁君是以君子終日行不離
輜重雖有榮觀燕處超然奈何萬乘之主
而以身輕天下輕則失臣躁則失君

Inner strength is the master
of all frivolities.
Tranquillity is the master
of all agitated emotions.

Those who succumb to frivolities
have lost their inner strength.
Those who succumb to agitated emotions
have lost their tranquillity

The wise cultivate
inner strength and tranquillity.
That is why they are not seduced
by addictive temptations.

Verse 27
WISDOM IS EFFORTLESS MUTUALITY

迷是謂要妙
善人善人之資不愛其資雖智大
故無棄物是謂龔明故善人不善人之師不
解是以聖人常善救人故無棄人常善救物
善閉無關楗而不可開善結無繩約而不可
善行無轍迹善言無瑕讁善計不用籌策

The expert traveler leaves no footprints.
The expert speaker makes no mispronunciations.
The expert in calculation needs no calculator.

The expert in closing things needs no lock,
yet not one can open what has been closed.
The expert in binding uses no knots,
yet no one can pull apart what has been bound.

The expert in caring for things never wastes anything.
The expert at helping people never abandons anyone.

These are the paths to enlightenment.
Those who arrive at their destination
teach those who are still on the path,
while those still on the path
are sources of wisdom for the teachers.

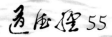

知其雄守其雌為天下谿為天下谿常德不
離復歸於嬰兒知其白守其黑為天下式為天
下式常德不忒復歸於無極知其榮守其辱
為天下谷為天下谷常德乃足復歸於樸散
則為器聖人用之則為官長故大制不割

28 THE FUSION OF OPPOSITES

To know the masculine and be true to the feminine
is to be the waterway of the world.

To be the waterway of the world is to flow with the Great Integrity,
always swirling back to the innocence of childhood.

To know yang and to be true to yin is
to echo the universe.

To echo the universe is to merge with the Great Integrity,
ever returning to the infinite.

To know praise and be true to the lowly
is to be a model for the planet.

To be a model for the planet is to express the Great Integrity
as the Primal Simplicity – like an uncarved block.

When the uncarved block goes to the craftsman,
it is transformed into something useful.

The wise craftsman cuts as little as necessary
because he follows the Great Integrity.

將欲取天下而為之者吾見其不得已天下神
器不可為也為者敗之執者失之故物或行
或隨或噓或吹或強或羸或載或隳是以聖
人去甚去奢去泰

29 WE ARE THE WORLD

Those who have most power and wealth
treat the planet as a thing to be possessed,
to be used and abused according to their own dictates.
But the planet is a living organism,
a Great Spiritual Integrity.

To violate this Integrity
is certain to cull forth disaster
since each and every one of us
is an inherent part
of this very organism.

All attempts to control the world
can only lead to its decimation
and to our own demise
since we are an inseparable part
of what we are senselessly trying to coerce.

Any attempt to possess the world
can only lead to its loss
and to our own dissolution
since we are an intrinsic part
of what we are foolishly trying to possess.

The world's pulse is our pulse.
The world's rhythms are our rhythms.
To treat our planet with care, moderation and love
is to be in synchrony with ourselves
and to live in the Great Integrity.

Verse

30 DEFENSE AND AGGRESSION

Those on the path of the Great Integrity
never use military force to conquer others.
Every aggressive act harvests its own counter-terrorism.

Wherever the military marches,
the killing fields lay waste to the land,
yielding years of famine and misery.

When attacked, those on the path of the Great Integrity
defend themselves benevolently,
never revenging.

Achieve success without arrogance,
without seeking glory,
and without violating others.

Aggression leaches our strength and humanity,
subverting the Great Integrity,
and inviting disaster.

以道佐人主者不以兵強天下其事好還師之
所處荊棘生焉大軍之後必有凶年故善
者果而已不敢以取強焉果而勿
伐果而勿驕果而不得已果而勿強物壯則
老是謂不道不道早已

道德經 61

夫佳兵者不祥之器物或惡之故有道者不
處君子居則貴左用兵則貴右兵者不祥之
器非君子之器不得已而用之恬淡為上勝
而不美而美之者是樂殺人夫樂殺人者不可
得志於天下矣吉事尚左凶事尚右是以偏將
軍處左上將軍處右言居上勢則以喪禮
處之殺人眾多則以悲哀泣之戰勝則以喪
禮處之道常無名樸雖小天下莫能臣侯王

Verse 31 WAR

The finest weapons are the worst evils.
They are universally loathed.
Therefore, help guide your nation to the non-aggressive path.

The wise hold steady on the passive yin path.
Those who are aggressive prefer the active yang.

Weapons are instruments of coercion and devils of death.
Resort to them only in dire necessity.
Peace is our natural state of being.

If weapons must be wielded to defend ourselves,
and we are victorious, never rejoice.
Can there be joy over the slaughter of others?

On joyous occasions,
we attune with the yang side.
On sad occasions, with the yin.

During battle, the soldiers are on the left yang side,
engaging in the combat.
The commanders are on the right yin side,
observing the action.

After the battle, the soldiers who have slain others,
move to the yin side and mourn,
while the commanders, now on the yang side,
are celebrating victory even though it is a funeral.

32

IS IT NOT TIME TO UNIFY THE FRAGMENTS?

Although the Great Integrity is infinite,
and therefore undefined,
it is silent in its Primal Simplicity.

Nothing is its superior.
When humanity embraces the Great Integrity,
all life on earth will be grateful.

All yin and yang will be harmonized
in the sweet daily dew, and peace will reign
on the planet without anyone commanding it.

When the Primal Simplicity atomized
into the 10,000 fragments, with their 10,000 names,
our planet became endangered.

Now – are there not enough fragments?
Is it not time to stop and return to the universal sea
from which all streams emerged?

To return to the Great Integrity
is to obliterate
the list of the 10,000 endangered species.

江海也 莫之令而自均始制有名名亦既有夫亦將知 若能守萬物將自賓天地相合以降甘露人 以知止所以不殆譬道之在天下猶川谷之於

道德經 65

33 WHO ARE YOU?

If you understand others, you are astute.
If you understand yourself, you are insightful.

If you master others, you are uncommonly forceful.
If you master yourself you have uncommon inner strength.

If you know when you have enough, you are wealthy.
If you carry your intentions to completion, you are resolute.

If you find your roots and nourish them, you will know longevity.
If you live a long creative life, you will leave an eternal legacy.

壽 之者當強行者有志不失其所久死而不亡者

知人者智自知者明勝人者有力自勝者強知

道德經 67

34 HUMILITY AND GREATNESS

The Great Integrity is unboundable like a flood.
It cannot be manipulated this or that way.
It is the very wellspring of life,
always outpouring, never commanding.

Although the source for every need,
it is never demanding.
It does its work silently
and unpretentiously.

All return to the Great Integrity
as our liberating universal home.
By never seeking greatness,
greatness permeates in deed.

大道汎兮其可左右萬物恃之以生而不辭功
成不居衣被萬物而不為主故常無欲可名
於小矣萬物歸焉而不知主可名於大矣是
以聖人能成其大也以其不自大故能成其大

THE CONSUMMATE FOOD
AND THE ULTIMATE MUSIC

執大象天下往往而不害安平泰樂與餌過
客止道之出口淡乎其無味視之不足見聽之
不足聞用之不可既

When you merge with the universe,
the whole world is attracted to you,
discovering through you
its own security, peace and good health.

Passing guests may stop by—at first attracted
to your savory food and inspirational music.
But they might leave more deeply enriched
than they could have anticipated—

Because the silent song of Tao
is the ultimate music,
and the infinite delicacy of Tao
is the consummate nourishment.

將欲歙之必固張之將欲弱之必固強之將欲

廢之必固興之將欲奪之必固與之是謂微明

柔弱勝剛強魚不可脫於淵國之利器不

可以示人道常無為而無不為侯王若能守萬

What is overexpanded becomes diminished.
What is too strong becomes weakened.
What is too high is cut down.
What is overpossessed becomes impoverished.

It is in the nature of process that in the final stages,
those who are overextended,
overarmed and overprivileged,
shall be overcome.

Disaster stalks the fish
which swims up from its deep water home,
and the army which threatens to conquer
those beyond its own borders.

The Great Integrity imposes no action,
yet it leaves nothing undone.
Were governments to embrace it,
everything would develop naturally.

If thereafter an old ego should reincarnate,
the already permeated Primal Simplicity
would neutralize it in its pervasive silence.

Returning to silence is returning to peace.
Returning to peace, the world reharmonizes itself.

名之樸亦將不欲不欲以靜天下將自正

物將自化而欲作吾將鎮之以無名之樸無

上德不德是以有德下德不失德是以無德上
德無為而無以為下德為之而有以為上仁為
之而無以為上義為之而有以為上禮為之而莫
之應則攘臂而仍之故失道而後德失德而後
仁失仁而後義失義而後禮夫禮者忠信之薄
而亂之首也前識者道之華而愚之始也是以
大丈夫處其厚不處其薄居其實不居其
華故去取彼此

You can readily recognize the highest virtuousness
because it never places itself on display.
You can readily recognize the lowest virtuousness
because it is always announcing itself.

The highest virtue quietly serves universal needs.
The lowest virtue actively strives for personal success.
The highest morality serves common needs.
The lowest morality is self-serving.

True benevolence
acts without intention.
But when rituals go unheeded,
they are enforced with rolled-up sleeves.

Failing the Great Integrity, we resort to virtuousness.
Failing virtuousness, we resort to moralizing.
Failing moralizing, we resort to dogma,
the most superficial form of faith and loyalty,
and the nourishment for confusion.

Natural persons are attracted
to substance rather than form,
to the nutritious fruit rather than the enticing flower,
to that which dwells deeply within,
rather than to that which clings superficially to the surface.

昔之得一者天得一以清地得一以寧神得一
以靈谷得一以盈萬物得一以生侯王得一以
為天下貞其發之一也天無以清將恐裂地無
以寧將恐發神無以靈將恐歇谷無以盈將
恐竭萬物無以生將恐滅侯王無以為貞而貴
高將恐蹶故貴以賤為本高以下為基是以侯
王自稱孤寡不穀此其以賤為本耶非乎
故致數譽無譽不欲琭琭如玉落落如石

Verse
39 THEN AND NOW

In ancient times, all entities had their own integrity and function.
The sky was clear and endless.
The earth was calm and firm.
The gods were charged with spiritual powers.
The wells were clean and full.
The 10,000 creatures were healthy and fecund.
Leaders were elected to plan the work and defense of the community.
How wondrously concordant!

If the sky were not endless, it could have fallen.
If the earth were not firm, it could have burst.
If the gods did not exercise their spiritual powers,
they would have been abandoned.
If the wells were not full, they could have dried up.
If the 10,000 creatures were not productive,
they could have become extinct.
If the leaders did not plan the work and defense of the community,
they would have been replaced.
In this way, each entity had its own essentiality,
each part complementing every other.

Nowadays, when the privileged among us identify themselves
with the orphan, the widower and the hungry one,
it may be an opportunistic appeal for the support of the lowly,
or a realization that loudly trumpeting self-glory negates itself,
or a premonition that shining like jade, and resounding like stone chimes
attracts the desperate adventurers among those deprived of hope,
inviting disaster among those who create these deprivations.

反者道之動
弱者道之用天下之物生於有

有生於無

The movement of the Great Integrity is infinite,
yet its character is passive.
Being defines every form of life,
yet all originate in, and return to, non-being.

上士聞道勤而行之中士聞道若存若亡下
士聞道大笑之不笑不足以為道故建言
有之明道若昧進道若纇進道若退上德
若谷大白若辱廣德若不足建德若偷質
真若渝大方無隅大器晚成大音希聲大
象無形道隱無名夫惟道善貸且成

When most people hear about the Great Integrity,
they waiver between belief and disbelief.
When wise people hear about the Great Integrity,
they diligently follow its path.
When ignorant people hear about it
they laugh out loud!
By this very laughter, we know its authenticity.

It is said that –
enlightenment appears dark,
the progressive way appears retrograde,
the smooth way appears jagged,
the highest peak of revelation appears empty like a valley,
the cleanest appears to be soiled,
the greatest abundance appears insufficient,
the most enduring inner strength appears like weakness,
and creativity appears imitative.

Great talents mature slowly.
Great sounds are silent.
Great forms look shapeless.
Transcendent squareness has no corners.

The Great Integrity hides behind all forms,
stubbornly nourishing the paradoxes that can enlighten us.

道生一一生二二生三三生萬物萬物負陰而抱
陽沖氣以為和人之所惡唯孤寡不穀而王公
以為稱故物或損之而益或益之而損人之所
教亦我義教之強梁者不得其死吾將以為
教父

42 THE PRINCIPLES OF TRANSFORMATION

The Great Integrity expresses one.
One manifests as two.
Two is transformed into three.
And three generates all the myriad entities of the universe.

Every entity always returns to yin after engaging yang.
The fusion of these two opposites
births the Vital Energy that sustains the harmony of life.

But for most people, this harmony is decimated
by inheriting a condition
of relative misery, scarcity and victimization.

Politicians cleverly pretend that they too originate
from the toxic soil of this misery,
even while designing the very laws
that legitimate victimization.

But watch out – those who hoard oversufficiency
will be diminished!
And those who are diminished
will become bountiful!

These commonly known truths
that common people teach each other,
are also my truths.

As you sow, so shall you reap.
Such is the heart of my teaching
in a world forced to live heartlessly.

43 THE VALUE OF MINIMUMS

That which is most tender
can overcome that which is most rigid.
That which has least substance
can penetrate that which has least space.

Acting without deliberate action,
and teaching without uttering a word
are rarely practiced.
So few find their way to the Great Integrity!

天下之至柔馳騁天下之至堅無有入於無間
吾是以知無為之有益不言之教無為之益天
下希及之

名與身孰親身與貨孰多得與亡孰病是故
甚愛必大費多藏必厚亡知足不辱知止不
殆可以長久

Which do you value more –
your wealth or your wellness?
Which is more harmful –
to lead or to lose?

The greater is your attachment,
the more bereft is your release.
The more you hoard,
the less is left to enjoy.

Those on the path
to the Great Integrity
flow without forcing,
leaving no space for disasters.

大成若缺其用不敝大盈若沖其用不窮大

直若屈大巧若拙大辯若訥躁勝寒靜勝

熱清靜為天下正

Completeness can seem incomplete,
yet the completeness that we achieve can be remarkable.
Fullness can seem empty,
yet the fullness that we achieve can be very useful.

Truth can appear as lie.
Straightness can appear as twisted.
Skillfulness can appear to be clumsy.
Eloquence can sound like foolishness.

But the dialectic of yin and yang is not illusory.
Activity can overcome cold.
Tranquillity can overcome heat.
And peacefulness is the natural seed of a violent world.

天下有道却走馬以糞天下無道戎馬生於
郊罪莫大於可欲禍莫大於不知足咎莫大
於欲得故知足之足常足矣

Verse
46 ENOUGH IS ENOUGH!

When the Great Integrity permeated our lives,
freely galloping horses fertilized the fields.

When the Great Integrity was lost,
war horses were bred in the countryside.

There is no greater calamity
than acquisitiveness racing out of control.

Only those who know when enough is enough
can ever have enough.

不出戶知天下不闚牖見天道其出彌遠其
知彌少是以聖人不行而知不見而名無為而
成

We can understand the world as it is
without leaving our home.
We can understand the world as it might be
without peering dreamily out our window.

The further we go,
the less we know.

Wise people understand the 10,000 things
without going to each one.
They know them without having to look at each one,
and they transform all without acting on each one.

Verse 48 · ALL IS DONE WITHOUT DOING

為學日益為道日損損之又損以至於無為
無為而無不為矣故取天下者常以無事及
其有事不足以取天下

To obtain a diploma requires the storage of trivia.
To obtain the Great Integrity requires their abandonment.

The more we are released from vested fragments of knowledge,
the less we are compelled to take vested actions,
until all is done without doing.

When the ego interferes
in the rhythms of process,
there is so much doing!
But nothing is done.

道德經 97

Verse

49 WISDOM

Wise people are not absorbed
in their own needs.
They take the needs of all people as their own.

They are good to the good.
But they are also good to those
who are still absorbed in their own needs.

Why?
Because goodness is in the very nature
of the Great Integrity.

Wise people trust
those who trust.
But they also trust those who do not trust.

Why?
Because trusting is in the very nature
of the Great Integrity.

Wise people merge with all others
rather than stand apart judgmentally.
In this way, all begin to open their ears and hearts,
more prepared to return to the innocence of childhood.

聖人無常心以百姓心為心善者吾善之不善
者吾亦善之德善矣信者吾信之不信者吾
亦信之德信矣聖人之在天下惵惵為天下
渾其心百姓皆注其耳目聖人皆孩之

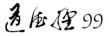

出生入死生之徒十有三死之徒十有三人之
生動之死地亦十有三夫何故以其生生之厚
蓋聞善攝生者陸行不遇兕虎入軍不被
甲兵兕無所投其角虎無所措其爪兵無所

50 THE FORCES OF LIFE AND DEATH

Every one of us is born,
And everyone dies.

However, three of every ten
seem to be born to live,
three seem to be born to die,
and three live lifefully or deathfully
according to their chosen life styles.

But only one in ten
seems to survive all dangers.
When walking through the jungle,
she never fears the rhinoceros
because there seems to be no place in her to butt his horns.
She never fears the tiger
because there seems to be no place to sink his claws,
and she never fears weapons
because there seems to be no place their steel can penetrate.

This is the fulfilled person of the Great Integrity
who leaves no space in life for premature death.

容其刃夫何故以其無死地道生之德畜之
物形之勢成之是以萬物莫不尊道而貴
德道之尊德之貴夫莫之爵而常自然
故道生之畜之長之育之成之熟之養之
覆之生而不有為而不恃長而不宰是謂
玄德

51 NATURAL BIRTHING

All in the universe derive from the Primal Integrity.
The interaction of yin and yang shapes and nourishes them,
and evolution ever transforms them
in their endless ecological dance.

Therefore, in its own way,
every entity celebrates its Primal Mother.
Not out of any mandate.
Not out of any obligation.
But solely as the expression of its own integrity.

天下有始以為天下母既得其母以知其子既知
其子復守其母没身不殆塞其兑閉其門終
身不勤開其兑濟其事終身不救見小曰
明守柔曰強用其光復歸其明無遺身殃
是謂龍常

52 RETURNING TO OUR ORIGINS

Everything has a common origin
that we might call the Mother of the Universe.

Once in pre-conscious times, we were all a part of this Mother,
just as we—all her children—were part of each other.

This was when we were all umbilically still attached
to the Great Integrity.

Some thousands of years ago, our species alone
issued a declaration of independence from our Mother.
Now it is time to reunite with her.

Thereafter, we will never any more suffer the 10,000 miseries
that only we human beings have acquired.

Block all the loopholes! Shut all the doors to the old temptations!
And we will never again feel deprived.

If we crawl through the loopholes, if we race through the gate
back to the 10,000 addictions, we will never be fulfilled.

How shall we know the Great Integrity?
When our insights proliferate even in the smallest matters.
When our strength is boundless even while ever yielding.

We can keep our outsights when returning to our insights.
In this way, we will reharmonize with our Mother,
celebrating the Great Integrity on a higher level.

Verse
53 NOT YET ON THE WAY

Those who have the smallest grain of wisdom
would want to walk the simple path of the Great Integrity.
Their only fear would be to go astray.

Indeed, there is a good reason to fear
when most of the world is piled into two wagons
racing toward each other on a single lane road.

In one over-crowded wagon is the vast majority
who live in weedy fields
with empty granaries.

In the other wagon are those
whose garments are opulently embroidered.
They gorge themselves
on rich foods far beyond their appetites,
and guzzle their inebriating drinks far beyond their thirst.

They accumulate wealth
even beyond their avaricious cravings
while armed to the teeth against their starving neighbors.

Surely such thievish degradation
couldn't be the way to the Great Integration.

使我介然有知行於大道唯施是畏大道甚

夷而民好徑朝甚除田甚蕪倉甚虛服文

彩帶利劍厭飲食資財有餘是謂盜夸

非道也哉

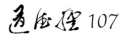 107

善建者不拔善抱者不脫子孫祭祀不輟脩之
身其德乃真脩之家其德乃餘脩之鄉其德乃
長脩之國其德乃豐脩之天下其德乃普故
以身觀身以家觀家以鄉觀鄉以國觀國以
天下觀天下吾何以知天下之然哉以此

Verse 54 THE WHOLE IS IN EACH PART

Whatever is planted deeply is not easily uprooted.
Whatever is embraced sincerely does not crave escape.
Ever since we lost our intuition as our main guide in life,
these virtues have had to be consciously cultivated to survive.

Cultivate them in yourself and they will be genuine.
Cultivate them in your family and they will surely flourish.
Cultivate them in your community and they will be long lasting.
Cultivate them in your country and they will be widely propagated.
Cultivate them in the world and they will certainly become universal.

In this way you will know others by what you do yourself.
You will know families by what you contribute as a family.
You will know the world by what you do as a planetary citizen.

How do we know all this?
Because we know that each part is the whole,
and the whole is in each part.

THE PROMISES OF THE GREAT INTEGRITY

When we will live in complete integrity,
we will be innocent like newborn babies.
Wasps and scorpions will not sting us.
Wild beasts will not maul us.
Birds of prey will not seize us.

Our bones will be pliable, our sinews soft.
Yet our grip will be firm.
Even before we have known conjugality,
our sexuality will be easily aroused
because we will be so virile.

We'll sing all day long without becoming hoarse
because we'll be in full harmony.
To be in harmony
is to live in the Great Integrity.
To live in the Great Integrity is the ultimate wisdom.

However, to interfere with nature is to seek control.
To seek control is to create dis-stress.
To create dis-stress produces exhaustion.
All these negations of the Great Integrity
also negate life and its longevity.

含德之厚比於赤子毒蟲不螫猛獸不據攫
鳥不搏骨弱筋柔而握固未知牝牡之合而峻
作精之至也終日號而嗌不嗄和之至也知和曰常
知常曰明益生曰祥心使氣曰強物壯則老是
謂不道不道早已

Those who know don't lecture.
Those who lecture don't know.

To prepare the way for the Great Integrity—
Close the rationalizing routes!
Shut the gloomy gates!
Blunt the sharp edges!
Release those who are tethered!
Soften the blinding lights!
Unite the world!

We cannot achieve the Great Integrity
through intimacy or emotional detachment,
nor through posturing or humility.

Since the Great Integrity makes no judgments or demands,
how will we know when it has arrived?
When it permeates us with its universal "is-ness".

知者不言言者不知塞其兌閉其門挫其銳解
其紛和其光同其塵是謂玄同不可得而親不
可得而疎不可得而利不可得而害不可得而
貴故為天下貴

113

SIMPLICITY BLOSSOMS
WHEN COERCION DIES

Govern a state with predictable actions.
Fight a war with surprise attacks.
But the universe becomes ours
only by eliminating coercive acts.
By not doing, nothing lacks.

How do we know these lessons?
By tuning into our Essence.

The more taboos and prohibitions there are,
the poorer the people become.
The more deadly weapons there are,
the more our fears turn us numb.

When craftiness spreads far,
the more bizarre what is done,
The stricter the laws there are,
the less the robbers run.

Therefore, the wise know
to make no one a foe.
The less coercing we do,
The more tranquillities grow.

When harmony reigns,
and we rule ourselves with felicity,
everyone gains,
and we'll all live in simplicity.

以正治國以奇用兵以無事取天下吾何以知此

然哉以此天下多忌諱而民彌貧民多利器國

家滋昏人多伎巧奇物滋起法令滋彰盜賊

多有故聖人云我無為而民自化我好靜而民

自正我無事而民自富我無欲而民自樸我

無情而民自清

Verse 58 ALTERNATIVES

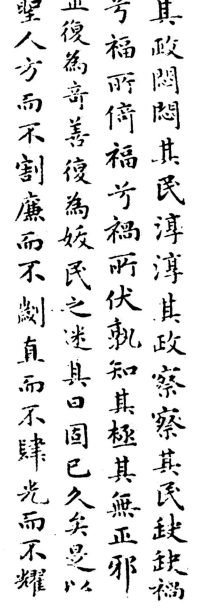

When a government is more benign,
the people are more productive.
When a government is more tyrannical,
the people are more rebellious.

But whatever the government,
if disaster is the bitter fruit of others' good fortune,
how long can such injustice be tolerated?
How long we have endured the hypocrisies!

Those pretending to be righteous act deceitfully.
Those pretending to be religious revert to evil.
We have been deluded!
And each day it becomes worse!

Be firm and armed, but do no harm!
Be as sharp as a knife, but do not cut!
Be ready to transform, but do not provoke!
Illuminate the darkness of ignorance, but do not blind!

Verse 59 THE IMPORTANCE OF MODERATION

To serve humanity,
there is nothing more important
than to be moderate.

To be moderate
is to return to the female yin principle.

To return to the yin
is to become nurturing.

To be nurturing
is to acquire enormous capacity.

To have enormous capacity
is to be ready for the Great Integrity

To be ready for the Great Integrity
is to be ready to serve humanity.

In this way we will become firmly planted
in the Great Integrity,
the pathway to a clear vision and a long life.

治人事天莫如嗇夫是謂早復早復謂之重積
德重積德則無不克無不克則莫知其極莫
知其極可以有國之母可以長久是謂深根
固蔕長生久視之道

119

治大國以烹小鮮以道莅天下者其鬼不神
非其鬼不神其神不傷人聖人亦不傷人夫
兩不相傷故德交歸焉

60 OUR FUTURE

Govern a country like you would fry a small fish –
with care, respect and with the least interference.

When the world is governed according to the Great Integrity,
evil will lose its power.

Not only will evil lose its power,
it will no longer even exist.

When evil ceases to exist,
neither will good exist.

Without good and evil,
we simply will live totally in our human natures.

No one will compromise anyone else
because we will all be inextricable parts of the Great Integrity.

In our era,
when the Great Integrity has been lost,
separate states have arisen.
Some become very large.
Others remain very small.

When the larger ones
try to conquer the small,
at first the smaller ones are defeated
even though yang aggression
meets yang resistance.
But death stalks the people
on both sides of war.

Is it not better for great countries
to be like vast low lying lands
into which all streams passively go?

And the smaller countries,
like the innocent streams,
can be welcomed
at the end of their passage
by wide open arms,
calmly receiving their flow?

Would not this mutual humility
save countless lives now,
while serving as a rehearsal
for the coming of the Tao?

大國者下流天下之交天下之牝常以靜勝
牝以靜為下故大國以下小國則取小國以
下大國則取大國故或下以取或下而取大國
不過欲無畜人小國不過欲入事人兩者各
得其所欲故大者宜為下

道者萬物之輿善人之寶不善人之所保美言
可以市尊行可以加人人之不善何棄之有故
立天子置三公雖有拱璧以先駟馬不如坐進
此道古之所以貴此道者何也不曰求以得有
罪以免耶故為天下貴

62 REHEARSALS FOR THE GREAT INTEGRITY

The Great Integrity is the sanctuary
of all human beings.

For those who are honest and caring,
it is a guide and a treasure.

For those who are dishonest and deceitful,
it is also a treasure
because a good word can rationalize a selfish act,
and because a good act, now and then,
can serve as a mask for living extravagantly
from the misery of others.

Since the Great Integrity is so universally acknowledged,
don't cast away those who use it opportunistically.
Rather cast away the opportunities to live selfishly
so that the Great Integrity
can more fully permeate all our lives.

We might begin
with the inauguration ceremonies of our leaders.
Instead of showering them with precious gifts,
instead of the public swearing of meaningless oaths,
why not share a meditation on the Great Integrity
as a prelude to its comprehensive embrace?

Verse 63 THE SECRETS OF GETTING THINGS DONE

為無為事無事味無味大小多少報怨以德
圖難於其易為大於其細天下之難事必
作於易天下之大事必作於細是以聖人終不
為大故能成其大夫輕諾必寡信多易必多
難是以聖人猶難之故終無難矣

Act without acting on.
Work without working at.

Enter bountifulness when it is still insufficiency.
Answer with kindness when faced with hostility.

Begin a difficult task in its easy stage
because large problems grow from small ones.

Begin a large task in its formative state
because complex issues originate from simple ones.

But beware of those who promise quick and easy solutions!
Accept problems as challenges.

In this way, the sage accomplishes great tasks
without ever having to struggle with them.

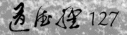

其安易持其未兆易謀其脆易泮其微易
散為之於未有治之於未亂合抱之木生於
毫末九層之臺起於累土千里之行始於足
下為者敗之執者失之是以聖人無為故無敗
無執故無失民之從事常於幾成而敗之慎
終如始則無敗事矣是以聖人欲不欲不貴難
得之貨學不學復眾人之所過以輔萬物之
自然而不敢為

It is easy to hold
what is still stable.
It is easy to mold
what is not yet formed.

It is easy to shatter
what is still fragile.
It is easy to scatter
what is yet light and small.

Therefore, act now rather than wait.
Get things done before it's too late.

A huge tree that you can't get your arms around
 grows from a tiny seedling birth.
A tower of nine stories high
rises from a small heap of earth.

A thousand mile journey begins with one step.
This is an ancient tale.
Those who procrastinate,
and those who take premature actions fail.

Those who interfere in processes disrupt them.
Those who hold tightly to possessions lose everything.
Wise people succeed because they never force an outcome.
They never suffer a loss because they are not attached to anything.

Many succeed in gathering a few assets.
But when the stakes begin to sail, and
greed crashes through all cautionary boundaries,
failures unmercifully prevail.

Wise people don't accumulate possessions,
or teach anyone to amass things.
They devote themselves to the natural rhythms
that the Great Integrity brings.

古之善為道者，非以明民，將以愚之。民之難治，以其智多。故以智治國，國之賊；不以智治國，國之福。知此兩者亦楷式。能知楷式，是謂玄德。玄德深矣遠矣，與物反矣，然後乃至大順。

Verse

65 THE LOSS OF INNOCENCE

In ancient times,
before there were those who were governed,
and those who governed over,
the sage blended with others,
and all was done through the Primal Simplicity.
People lived in innocence.

When the Great Fragmentation
replaced the Great Integrity,
cleverness defeated wisdom.
Even some enlightened sages
became victims of the rulers
commanding the highest intrigue.

Why do all the hundreds of great rivers
flow naturally to the sea?
Because the sea is always lower than the rivers.

When are thousands of people attracted to a sage?
When she positions herself below them,
always listening, tirelessly responding to their needs.

Never commanding.
Never coercing.
Never manipulating.

Such a sage is forever adored.
Since she treats everyone with love and respect,
everyone loves and respects her.

江海所以能為百谷王者以其善下之也故能為
百谷王是以聖人欲上人以其言下之欲先人以
其身下之是以聖人處上而人不重處前而人不
害是以天下樂推而不厭以其不爭故天下莫
能與之爭

133

天下皆謂我道大似不肖夫惟大故似不肖

若肖久矣其細矣夫我有三寶保而持之一曰慈

二曰儉三曰不敢為天下先夫慈故能勇儉故

能廣不敢為天下先故能成器長今捨其

慈且勇捨其儉且廣捨其後且先死矣夫慈

以戰則勝以守則固天將救之以慈衛之

Verse 67 THE THREE TREASURES

When most people hear about the Great Integrity, they say it is useless folly.
Because it is not like anything in the world we know, they also find it inconceivable.

On the contrary!
The Great Integrity has given us three treasures to cherish:
The first is love.
The second is moderation.
The third is humility.

If you love, you will be fearless.
If you are moderate, you might always sense abundance in life.
If you live in humility, you will be widely trusted.

But you will not have the capacity to love if you are fearful.
Even worse, if you are fearless and without love, you will always be courting disaster.

If you live in insufficiency, you have no opportunity to be moderate.
If you live in overabundance, you not only live immoderately,
but are always courting disaster.

If no one trusts you, then compensatory ego will preclude humility.
If everyone trusts you, and you lack humility, you will always court disaster.

The three treasures are practical guides to the Great Integrity.
The greatest foolishness is to live without them.

Verse 68 THE ETHICS OF WAR

力是善善善
是謂用人者為士
謂配人者為者不者
配天之下武不武
天古德是善怒善
古之是謂勝善戰
之極謂不敵勝者
極　用爭者敵不
　　人之不者怒
　　之德爭不
　　　是　爭

The best soldier fights
without vengeance,
without anger
and without hate.

He puts himself humbly
below his comrades,
thereby eliciting
the highest loyalty from them.

This is the power
of non-belligerence
and cooperation.
It is the ancient path to the Great Integrity.

道德經 137

69 IN WAR THE DEFENDER
WILL BE VICTORIOUS

There is a saying
among those wise in military affairs:
"We do not act as host taking the initiative,
but would rather be the guest
assuming the defensive posture.
Rather than advancing one inch,
we would rather retreat one foot."

This is called
advancing without moving,
rolling up one's sleeves without baring one's arms,
fighting without weapons,
capturing the enemy without attacking.

There is no greater disaster
than boasting of one's invincibility.
Such boasts lead to the loss of the Three Treasures.
Therefore, when two opposing sides
meet in battle,
the one without an enemy
will be victorious.

用兵有言吾不敢為主而為客不敢進寸而
退尺是謂行無行攘無臂仍無敵執無兵
禍莫大於輕敵輕敵者幾喪吾寶故抗兵
加衷者勝矣

139

The Great Integrity is so easy to understand,
and so easy to practice.
Yet it is not understood.
Nor is it practiced.

It is not understood
because people's heads are filled
with 10,000 trivia and rationalizations,
leaving no space for anything else.

It is not practiced
because people are kept busy, though bored,
with the 10,000 corruptions and miseries
that leave no time for the Three Treasures.

The Great Integrity is so ancient,
as old as the universe itself!
How can we expect people to remember it
after so many millennia of repression?

That is why
sages dress in rags
while they wear the Three Treasures
deep inside their hearts.

吾言甚易知甚易行天下莫能知莫能行
言有宗事有君夫惟無知是以不我知也知
我者希則我貴矣是以聖人被褐懷玉

141

知不知上不知知病夫惟病病是以不病聖
人不病以其病病是以不病

Academia confuses knowledge with knowing.
Most everyone applauds the memorization of the 10,000 trivia.
Beware! These schooled addictions are not just myths—
They are a form of mental illness.

Any fragment of the mind,
divorced from heart, spirit, human community,
and from the primal reality of the universe,
is an abomination of the Great Integrity.

Let us prepare for the Great Integrity
by cleansing ourselves of all these cobwebs
of cluttered fragments that paralyze the mind.
In this way we will function as our own holistic physicians

Verse 72 COMPARING COERCIVE POWER AND THE EMPOWERMENT OF THE GREAT INTEGRITY

When people no longer fear the power of governments,
a far greater empowerment appears—
the Great Integrity—
which never needs to enforce itself.

Then, we will never again be driven from our homes
or be compelled to labor for the benefit of others.
We will all work naturally to fulfill ourselves,
and to meet our community needs.

In the Great Integrity,
we will all love ourselves and all others,
not as compensations for ego deprivations and defilements,
but as natural expressions of our humanity.

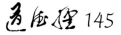 145

COURAGE, PATIENCE
AND PARADOXES

勇於敢則殺勇於不敢則活此兩者或利或害天之所惡孰知其故是以聖人猶難之天之道不爭而善勝不言而善應不召而自來繟然而善謀天網恢恢疎而不失

*The world we live in
requires great courage and patience.*

*Those with great courage, but little patience,
tend to kill or be killed.*

*Those with great courage as well as great patience
will tend to survive.*

*But the Great Integrity never judges you
for whatever path you happen to take.*

*The Great Integrity never strives
but always fulfills itself,*

*Never is commanded
but always responds.*

*Never is summoned
but always appears.*

*Never is impatient
but all is done on time.*

民常不畏死奈何以死懼之若使民常畏死
而為奇者吾得執而殺之孰敢常有司殺者殺
而代司殺者殺是謂代大匠斲夫代大匠斲
希有不傷其手矣

People do not fear death
when they are forced to live in hopeless misery,
Thereby the executioners are no threat
to fearless rebels who dare to make trouble.
They might even execute the executioners.

When people do fear death,
they do not defy the executioners at first.
But how long can the killings go on
before those who fear death
also become fearless?
Then, they too might execute the executioners.

By that time, the only ones left
who might serve as the executioners
would be the people themselves.
However, it is said that those who hew wood
in place of skilled carpenters
are likely to cut their own hands.

民之飢以其上食稅之多是以飢民之難治以其
上之有為是以難治民之輕死以其上求生之厚
是以輕死夫惟無以生為者是賢於貴生

Why are the people so hungry?
Because their grain is devoured
by the rich in taxes.
That is why the people are starving.

Why are the people so rebellious?
Because the government deprives them
of their liberties and rights.
That's why the people are rebellious.

Why do the people not fear death?
Because their lives
are made so miserable
that death seems no worse than life.

Thus, no one can enjoy the treasures of life—
neither the rich who squander their humanity,
nor the government which tyrannizes the people,
nor the people who have nothing to gain from life.

LET YIN PREDOMINATE OVER YANG

When we are born,
we are soft and supple.
But when we've perished
there's no more tenderness
to be cherished.

When plants are young,
they are pliant and fragile.
When they die,
as they lose their green,
they wither and dry.

The sharp sword and knife
tryst always with death,
while love without strife
is an ever devoted
disciple of life.

An inflexible army
seals its own fate.
When a tree branch grows brittle,
it easily snaps,
whether long or little.

Wherever you go,
the rigid lie low.
While the weightless in the sky,
and all that is gentle,
fly boundlessly high.

人之生也柔弱其死也堅強草木之生也柔脆
其死也枯槁故堅強者死之徒柔弱者生之徒
是以兵強則不勝木強則兵堅強處下柔弱
處上

The Way of the Great Integrity
is like stringing a bow,
pulling down the high,
lifting up the low–

Shortening the long,
lengthening the short
to take from the excessive
and give insufficiency support.

How opposite to our social norms
which increasingly impoverish the poor
to further enrich the rich
who do not need any more.

How can we gather the world's wealth
to create abundance for all in need?
Through rediscovering the Great Integrity,
by acting without praising the deed.

天之道其猶張弓乎高者抑之下者舉之有
餘者損之不足者補之天之道損有餘以補不
足人之道則不然損不足以奉有餘孰能損
有餘以奉不足於天下唯有道者是以聖人
為而不恃功成不處其不欲見賢耶

78 APPEARANCE AND REALITY

Nothing in the world
is softer and weaker than water.
Yet there is nothing better
for subduing all that is harder and stronger.

Everyone observes how weak overcomes strong,
how gentleness overcomes rigidity.
Yet, this principle is seldom put into conscious practice.

Though some may say it is useless
to accept responsibility
for the calamities and toxicities of the world,
taking such responsibility
might put us on the road to the Great Integrity.

Just remember that truth often masquerades as falsity,
and falsity as truth.

天下莫柔弱於水而攻堅強者莫之能勝以其
無以易之故柔勝剛弱勝強天下莫不知而莫
能行是以聖人云受國之垢是謂社稷主受國
不祥是謂天下王正言若反

Verse 79 THE TOXICITY OF BLAME

和大怨必有餘怨安可以為善是以聖人執左
契而不責於人故有德司契無德司徹天道
無親常與善人

Harboring a resentment
is sure to leave some resentment behind.
How can this be good?
It cannot.
Therefore, the wise accept all responsibility.

Although those who hold the power
keep blaming and bleeding the people,
the violated Great Integrity blames no one.
Once achieving the Great Integrity,
we will all function with a pure heart.

Verse 80 TRANSFORMING OUR LIVES

小國寡民使民有什伯之器而不用使民重死
而不遠徙雖有舟車無所乘之雖有甲兵無
所陳之使民復結繩而用之甘其食美其服
安其居樂其俗鄰國相望雞犬之聲相聞
民至老死不相往來

Let us fashion small states with few inhabitants
who, without stress,
can produce more than they require,
who are so happy with their lives
that they have no thought of migrating elsewhere –

Who inherit weapons and armor,
but no need to use them,
who return to honest forms of communication,
and the simple enjoyments
of an ecological way of life.

Although these states may be so close to each other
that they hear the barking of each other's dogs
and the crowing of each other's cocks,
living contentedly,
they will have no need to invade each other's space.

信言不美美言不信善者不辯辯者不善
知者不博博者不知聖人無積既以為人己愈
既以與人己愈多天之道利而不害人之道

Profound words are not clever.
Clever words are not profound.

Wise people are not quarrelsome.
Quarrelsome people are not wise.

Those who are intelligent are not ideologues.
Those who are ideologues are not intelligent.

The enlightened never hoard anything.
They share their possessions.

The more they give,
the greater their abundance.

The Great Integrity is the physician of the universe
who heals without harming and who acts without contention.

 *163*

Commentaries

ON THE VERSES

1 TRANSCENDING

The Tao that can be told
is not the universal Tao.
The name that can be named
is not the universal name.

In the infancy of the universe,
there were no names.
Naming fragments the mysteries of life
into ten thousand things
and their manifestations.

Yet mysteries and manifestations
spring from the same source:
The Great Integrity
which is the mystery within manifestation,
the manifestation within mystery,
the naming of the unnamed,
and the un-naming of the named.

When these interpenetrations
are in full attendance,
we will pass the gates of naming notions
in our journey toward transcendence.

COMMENTARY

We are not only reminded here that there is a dichotomy between the unnamed (our intuition) and the named (our reasoning), but also that these two seemingly opposite mind-worlds can be integral. Yet, *mysteries* (our intuition) and *manifestations* (our experience) spring from the same source: the Universal Tao (the Great Integrity) by which Lao Tzu means the wholeness and holiness that is embedded in our nature and in the entire nature of nature. Lao Tzu also reminds us of *the mystery within manifestation* (our intuition enriching our experience), *the manifestation within mystery* (our experience enriching our intuition), *the naming of the un-named* (the infusion of our reasoning consciousness with our intuitive consciousness), and *the un-naming of the named* (the dissolution of alienation from our reasoning consciousness).

What is implied here is nothing less than the healing of the split between the two hemispheres of our brain[1] which have become separated, alienated and at war with each other during the past few thousand years. Practically speaking, this means, for example, the "artistification" of science, the "scientification" of art, the "ecumenicalization" of religion, and the spiritualization of life.

In the realm of *science*, this is a process which nuclear physics, more than any other scientific discipline, has initiated. In a more advanced evolutionary stage, it will mean the transformation of our fixed and objective hierarchical structures into objective-subjective interactive processes. For example, our present linearly and hierarchically structured languages are likely to transform into a music-language, capable of communicating subtle differentiations and simultaneities of experience, reasoning and feeling.

In the realm of *art*, the Great Integrity implies the "artistification" of life and the gradual disappearance of our old age art "closets" such as museums and performance halls. In a more advanced evolutionary stage, we can imagine the transformation of musical and dance composition to improvisation, of painting framed pictures to the "artistification" of our entire environment.

In the realm of *religion*, we can look forward to the ecumenical dissolution of sects, dogmas and superstitions since they create a rigor mortis of the mind, emotions and spirit. In an even more advanced evolutionary stage we might achieve the spiritualization of every aspect of life and consciousness.

This verse welcomes the disappearance of all boundaries among art, science and religion as the walls and premises of every discipline dissolve into a higher consciousness and an uncompromising integrity of human relations and life experience. Therefore, *when these interpenetrations are in full attendance, we will pass the gates of naming notions in our journey toward transcendence.*

Verse 2 RELATIVITY

We know beauty because there is ugly.
We know good because there is evil.
Being and not being,
having and not having,
create each other.

Difficult and easy,
long and short,
high and low,
define each other,
just as before and after follow each other.

The dialectic of sound gives voice to music,
always transforming "is" from "was"
as the ancestors of "to be".

The wise teach without telling,
allow without commanding,
have without possessing,
care without claiming.

In this way we harvest eternal importance
because we never announce it.

COMMENTARY

This verse celebrates the relativity of reality, thereby aligning itself with modern science, especially Einstein's theory of relativity. The corollary is a rejection of fundamentalism and absolutism. *Verse 2* is a poetic reminder that one of our twenty-first century requisites is to transcend all superstitions. To believe that our world today is just as God created it and has never ever changed, nor will ever change, shuts the door to transformation. Such a premise locks us into the inequities of the past that were predicated on a condition of scarcity and a division between a minority who can fulfill their needs and a majority who cannot. twenty-first century technology makes *have* and *have-not* inequities, as well as their rationales, anachronistic.

Lao Tzu's theory of relativity suggests new paradigms of consciousness. He implies that when there will be no gluttony, there will be no starvation, when there will be no rich, there will be no poor. That is self-evident. However, what does it mean to say that when there will be no ugly, there will be no beauty, and that when there will be no evil, there will be no good?

It means that beauty and good will no longer be expressed as compensatory for the ugly and the evil in our life experience. It means that we will not any longer have to express *beauty* separated from life as art, nor *good* separated from life as a spiritual expression. It is possible that twenty-first century life will rediscover the harmony between our environment and us, and the harmony among each other, and within us.

It is this harmony that will be *good* and *beautiful* only as seen from our current perspective. But from a future perspective, *good* and *beautiful* as alienated compensations will not exist because evil and ugly will not exist. What we today call *good* and *beautiful* will simply permeate the character of life.

If *beauty* will no longer be separable from life, then we may expect that, eventually, there will no longer be concert halls and museums, since the music and art of life will be inherent in all the sounds, movements and patterns of ordinary life, and will be expressed by everyone of us, not just a specialist who creates beauty for us such as the professional musician and artist. We can imagine that some day every mode of communication with each other might be spontaneously musical and poetic, every movement we make might be a dance, every object we create – a visual delight, all expressing the integral and actualizing character of life.

Similarly, in the distant future, we may not have need for churches, temples and mosques since life itself may become spiritual in all its forms, activities and expressions. Compensatory religion may become as anachronistic as making our home in a cave. Clearly, when spirituality universally permeates life, the separate expression of particular sectarian religions may become only historical relics from an unholy past.

In such a world of the future, the teacher and the student might be so in tune with each other that *the wise* (will be able to) *teach without telling.*

Each of us may become so in tune with every other person that we may spontaneously *allow without commanding.* To the extent that our lives issue from material and spiritual abundance, will we be free to *have without possessing* and *care without claiming,* and because in this new condition, we can expect to give and receive love freely, our egos will no longer be starved. *In this way, we* (will) *harvest eternal importance because we* (will) *never* (need to) *announce it.*

Verse 3 TEMPERING

Overpraising the gifted
leads to contentiousness.
Overvaluing the precious
invites stealing.
Craving the desirable
loses contentment.

The natural person
desires without craving
and acts without excess.

By not doing,
everything is done.

COMMENTARY

Excess is rooted in deprivation. When our talents are not appreciated we endlessly seek praising. When we are denied the essentials of life, we overvalue the precious. When our physical, emotional and spiritual needs are unfulfilled, we develop desperate cravings because we are starved.

Freedom from deprivation will allow us to function effortlessly. Only then will everything be done as natural expressions of our life needs and rhythms rather than as compensations for our deprivations.

4 THE GREAT INTEGRITY

The Great Integrity is an endless abyss,
Yet, it is the inexhaustibly fertile
source of the universe.

It blunts all sharpness,
unties the entangled,
and merges with the dust!

Hidden but ever present –
this parent of the gods –
whose child may it be?

COMMENTARY

As the creator of all mythologies and realities, the Great Integrity (Tao) is the paradox that transcends all states of being. It is the *endless abyss, yet it is the inexhaustibly fertile source of the universe*. The Great Integrity is the mediator of every state. *It blunts all sharpness* and *unties the entangled*. It not only creates, transcends and modifies, but the Great Integrity itself *merges with the dust*, that state to which all matter ultimately returns.

In western theology nothing precedes God. But according to Lao Tzu, the Great Integrity is the *source of the universe*, including all ideas as well as the *10,000 phenomena*.[2] The gods are thereby also children of the Great Integrity. Lao Tzu goes on to ask the ultimate epistemological question: where did the Great Integrity come from – *whose child may it be?*

His implied answer is that beyond the finite limitations of our perceptions is an infinity of time, space, energy and matter, which, by definition, has no beginning. Therefore nothing precedes the Great Integrity, and it is nobody's child.

Such a concept transcends contemporary religion and science[3] both of which harness us to the quantified paradigms of the past few thousand years. The transcendence of these precepts is requisite to our entering the higher evolutionary phase that the twenty-first century promises as a potential for our species self-realization.

Verse

5 YIN AND YANG

Yin and yang aren't sentimental.
They exist without moralizing.
They act regardless of our wishes
within the ebb and flow
of every pregnant moment.

The space between yin and yang
is like a bellows –
empty, yet infinitely full.
The more it yields,
the more it fills.

Countless words
count less
than the silent balance
between yin and yang.

COMMENTARY

Yin and yang,[4] like heaven and earth, is a metaphor for all that exists. We are reminded here that existence is not sentimental. The course of events does not simply follow our wishes or prayers.

Moreover, the harder we try to force events to conform to our moralizations, the less likely our success. On the other hand, the more we yield to the rhythms (*bellows*) of life, the greater our fruition. How often Lao Tzu bids us to put aside our ideological predilections so that we may be free to ebb and flow with the new opportunities *of every pregnant moment*

Thus – *Countless words* (our exhortations) *count less than the silent* (existential) *balance between yin and yang.*

Verse

6 LIFE'S SPIRIT

The spirit of life
never dies.

It is the infinite gateway
to mysteries within mysteries.

It is the seed of yin,
the spark of yang.

Always elusive,
endlessly available.

COMMENTARY

The spirit of life is infinite, mysterious, inexhaustible and both passive (yin) and active (yang). It is the non-dualistic aspect of spirit that separates the Great Integrity from all religious precepts of spirit. There is a corollary separation of the Great Integrity from modern science, which also harbors dualistic premises.

However, twenty-first century meta-scientific spirituality is already seeded in molecular physics and in an ecumenical consciousness. Our twenty-first century opportunities are strewn with the materialization of the spiritual and the spiritualization of the material as we de-dichotomize all the cobwebs of our dualistic mythologies, allowing us to experience life as spontaneity and free of ideological filters.

Verse

7 MODESTY

The Great Integrity, having had no birth,
expresses its immortality
without pronouncements.

The wise are heard
through their silence,
always self-full through selflessness.

COMMENTARY

The ego is the issue here. It is the very act of calling attention to ourselves that alienates us from others. Moreover, it is this very alienation that prevents self and social fulfillments.

When we no longer have to respond to the compulsive alternating bulimic demands and anorexic sufferings of our battered egos, then we will fulfill ourselves naturally and silently just as the Great Integrity expresses its immortality without pronouncements.[5]

8 THE HIGHEST GOOD

The highest good is like water,
nourishing life effortlessly,
flowing without prejudice
to the lowliest places.

It springs from all
who nourish their community
with a benevolent heart as deep as an abyss,
who are incapable of lies and injustices,
who are rooted in the earth,
and whose natural rhythms of action
play midwife to the highest good
of each pregnant moment.

COMMENTARY

This verse defines the qualities of those who live in the highest goodness.

From an evolutionary point of view, we could differentiate four stages of goodness:

(1) The goodness that was expressed in the communality of tribal times, during which survival depended upon the total cooperation among all members of the tribe. During this *First Era* of human evolution,[6] goodness was the natural expression of both individual and social reality. "Badness", which was rare and a social anomaly, was defined as the violation of the tribal goodness norms (taboos) and usually punishable by excommunication from society.

(2) The goodness that Confucianism and other religions advocate as an expression of the more altruistic side of our personalities. The assumption in these advocacies is that goodness requires an effort, a struggle against our supposedly innate tendencies to be selfish and sinful. These "badness" characteristics came to be dominant during the *Second Era*[6] of human evolution that we euphemistically call *civilization*, during which the competitive economy of survival pitted us against each other.

(3) The goodness that is expressed in this verse which implies that while both goodness and badness coexist, that it is goodness that flows effortlessly like water, because it is goodness that is more at the core of nature, including human nature. To those of us who function as self-

appointed midwives to the transition from the *Second* to the *Third Era*, we define our *essential* selves as good rather than bad, that is, as innately concerned and loving rather than as selfish and ego-centered. We reach for this innate goodness as an antidote to our mis-educations in "badness" as we unearth the psychological roots for the rebirthing of our humanity.

(4) The goodness that transcends goodness when the polarization of good and bad will no longer exist. In its stead will be the consciousness and actualization of our inherent and socially educated humanity. It is only this fourth type of goodness that fully expresses the Great Integrity, and that we may postulate might define our lives in the far future *Third Era* of human evolution.[6]

Verse
9 OVERFULFILLMENT

Keep filling your bowl,
and it will spill over.

Keep sharpening your knife,
and it will blunt.

Keep hoarding gold in your house,
and you will be robbed.

Keep seeking approval,
and you will be chained.

The Great Integrity leads to actualization,
never overfulfillment.

COMMENTARY

Our culture conditions us to keep filling our bowl even after it is full, to keep accumulating more money even after we have enough to meet all our needs, to keep reaching out for more accolades even after we have been fully acknowledged.

No other species ever seeks more than it needs. To do so is a pathological symptom that negates the very fulfillments we crave. If we reject Freud's thesis that human beings are biologically self-destructive, what is the explanation for these self-negating behaviors?

When our bowl is the community bowl that we fill and use collectively, we never overfill it.

When our knife is the community knife that we sharpen and use together, we never oversharpen it.

When our possessions are community possessions that we gather and use for each other's mutual benefit, we never miserly hoard them.

When love is freely expressed, naturally nurturing each member of the community, we never seek it with insatiable desperation.

But in our culture, each of our bowls is our own bowl, competing with every other for filling. Each of our possessions is our own possession, acquired competitively in the heartless marketplace. Because we have sacrificed

177

9 OVERFULFILLMENT

cooperation for competition, *the cash-nexus* has taken the place of sharing mutual concern and love, generating instead – inequities, hostilities and inhumanities among us.

However, ours is that unique evolutionary moment when we can liberate ourselves from all the inequities of the past. One aspect of this liberation is the acquiring of a new Great Integrity consciousness that rejects the excesses of the past several thousand years. We can now transform our way of life so that we are no longer addicted to overfilling our bowls, over-sharpening our knives, over-accumulating possessions, and over-extending our demands for attention and love. Celebrate the Great Integrity as the pathway to actualization in which our self and social components will be mutually supportive and no longer in conflict with each other!

Verse
10 LIMITATIONS

When embracing the unity
of mind, body, emotions and spiritual being,
can we transcend our fragmentations
without leaving a trace?

When Qi Gong sculpts sinew suppleness,
can our flesh become soft as a new born babe?

Can we cleanse the inner vision,
leaving mind in spiritual purity?

Can our affairs of the heart,
and our affairs of state
be so unconditional
that we grant unqualified permissibility?

Can the gate to Yin be opened
without inviting Yang?

Can our reasoning mind be purged of coercion,
allowing our heart its unfettered joy?

Can we act like every other species,
seeking no reward,
taking no pride,
guiding without enslaving?

Such is our vision of the Great Integrity
on whose path we have at last planted
both feet,
ready to move, step by step,
until we arrive at the great unfettered gate.

COMMENTARY

There are two principal implications about our limitations in this hymn to the Great Integrity:

(1) The universal limitations of reality are relative rather than absolute. The answer to every question posed in this verse is therefore, *no* because nothing exists in its pure ideal form, and because there can be no yin without its opposite, yang.

(2) However, the conditions that define our time as the age of transition, lead us to answer these questions with a qualified, *yes*. We can now *begin* this journey, but our generations will never be able to fully actualize the Great Integrity. Specifically, we can begin the transformation from fragmentation to holism (stanza 1); from the shallow breath that hastens the aging of bodies to the Qi Gong[7] breath that rejuvenates us (stanza 2); from the superficial and toxic games our minds now play to the inner visions of our intuitive consciousness (stanza 3); from the typical manipulations and machinations of our intimate relations and our institutions to unconditional loving in our personal relations and non-coercive administration of our institutions (stanza 4); from a life whose decisions are generated by yang coercive commands to a life which flows through yin nurturing (stanza 5); from self-serving left brain[8] rationalization to a more holistic right brain joy (stanza 6); from a self-aggrandizing reward-seeking behavior to a more altruistically generated life style (stanza 7).

THE IMPORTANCE
OF WHAT IS NOT

We join thirty spokes
to the hub of a wheel,
yet it's the center hole
that drives the chariot.

We shape clay
to birth a vessel,
yet it's the hollow within
that makes it useful.

We chisel doors and windows
to construct a room,
yet it's the inner space
that makes it livable.

Thus do we
create what is
to use what is not.

COMMENTARY

It may seem that Lao Tzu in this verse advocates *what is not* over *what is*. Similarly, he seems to advocate *not doing* over *doing*.[9] It would appear that he announces *nothingness* as the goal of life. To make a pun, *nothing* could be further from his intent. In fact, he celebrates the maximal doing with the minimal effort.

Lao Tzu's *nothingness* is not a reference to the absence of content, but rather to the absence of aggression. He does not worship inaction, sleep, death or the withdrawal from a responsible life. In this verse, although he focuses on the inactive part as being most functional, clearly there would be no inactive part without having created the other parts. There is no center hole without making the spokes and hub, no hollow in the vessel without making the vessel, no inner space without constructing the walls, doors and windows that define it.

Lao Tzu rather reminds us that there is always a yin (the passive and empty component) that coexists with the yang (the active and shaping component). The two together provide the means to total action, total responsibility, *lifefulness*, and *lovefulness*. He focuses on the yin component in this verse as a metaphor for establishing the greater relative importance of nurturing (yin) compared with acting (yang), which is often expressed as aggression.

More specifically, the main reason we tend to forget or denigrate the yin part of all processes is that the yang part in our lives has become dominant and excessive, tending to express itself as coercion. This condition has defined our lives since ancient times. Only the forms of coercion have changed. But to divorce aggression from action does not leave emptiness, but the space for natural action, that action whose mother is our humanity and whose father is necessity, and which therefore is born in full innocence. Lao Tzu is an advocate of effortless effort and contentless content, paradoxes which imply that our experience of effort usually embraces coercion and the content of this effort is usually excessive.

We have lived in the bosom of manipulative relations so long that we can barely imagine work without the threat of unemployment, morality without the threat of God-given punishments, and honesty without the threat of laws and their enforcements. We are so uncompromisingly conditioned to these hegemonic relations that they seem to us like inherent expressions of reality rather than conditions that violate our human natures.

Can we imagine a world beyond wealth and poverty, power and powerlessness, health and sickness, beauty and ugliness, intelligence and stupidity, fullness and emptiness?[10] By placing our attention on the yin, Lao Tzu reminds us that there is such a soft natural world, and that we can enter it when we dissolve the power structures and premises that create these dichotomies. He reminds us that our humanity is beyond all these dichotomies, beyond all the separations that alienate us from nature, from each other and from our own nature.

Similarly, although enlightenment requires thoughtlessness as an emptying out process, Lao Tzu does not advocate emptying the mind as the ultimate goal, but rather as a means of cleansing it of its garbage and of preparing it for a more holistic, more human and less alienated content.[11]

This distinction between ends and means separates Lao Tzu's revolutionary leaps in consciousness from some fetishes, which mistake the cleansing processes for the ultimate goals. It is one thing to become aware of the hole in the wheel, the hollow in the glass, the space in the house; it is quite another to drive the chariot that has a hole, but no hub, to drink from the glass that has a hollow but nothing to contain it, or to live in a house that has space without walls. Lao Tzu's paradoxes transcend the myopic oversimplifications and rationalizations of the market mentality without ever sacrificing the down-to-earth practicalities of life.

Verse 12 CHOICES

Colors can make us blind!
Music can make us deaf!
Flavors can destroy our taste!
Possessions can close our options!
Racing can drive us mad
and its rewards obstruct our peace!

Thus, the wise
fill the inner gut
rather than the eyes,
always sacrificing the superficial
for the essential.

COMMENTARY

There is no intention here to sing the praises of asceticism. That idea is more in tune with Confucianism and Christianity.

Lao Tzu is mainly calling our attention to the relative importance of the inner compared with the outer, the essential compared with the superficial.

Furthermore, in excess, sights, sounds and flavors can destroy our senses. Certainly, our high profile crass billboards our violent TV and films, our high decibel junk music and denatured chemicalized "foods" qualify to make us blind and deaf, and to destroy our taste.

The last stanza spells it out without ambiguity by favoring the "inner gut", a metaphor for our *essentiality*, over the "eyes", a metaphor for our outer *superficiality*.

Verse 13 IDENTITY

Accolades can usher in
great trouble for your body.
Censure can herald misery.

Why can favor and disfavor
both be harmful?

Because both accolades and censure,
when filtered through self as ego,
always place us in jeopardy.

But when the universe becomes your self,
when you love the world as yourself,
all reality becomes your haven,
reinventing you as your own heaven.

Only then, will you transcend tense
to fully be here now.
Only then, no harm
will the universe proffer
nor you to her,
for you will be
not you but she
and both – the universal Great Integrity.

COMMENTARY

Both praise and criticism can result in harm when we relate to the world through an insatiable ego. That is because when so doing, each honor generates a need for an even greater honor, and each dishonor generates a lower self-esteem. In this way honoring and dishonoring both can result in dissatisfaction leading to a pathological state of body, mind, emotions and spirit.

However, when we identify ourselves as inextricable parts of the universe, rather than as our separate individual egos, accolades and criticisms, successes and failures, no longer have power over us, but are accepted as intrinsic and harmless aspects of participation in processes. The transformation from predominant ego-identity to predominant community-identity is one of our joyful pathways to the Great Integrity.

Verse

14 BEYOND REASON

That which we look at
but cannot see is the invisible.

That which we listen to
but cannot hear is the inaudible.

That which we reach for
but cannot grasp is the intangible.

Beyond reason,
   these three merge,
contradicting experience.

Their rising side isn't bright.
Their setting side isn't dark.

Sense-less, unnamable,
they return to the realms of nothingness.

Form without form,
image without image,
indefinable, ineluctable, elusive.

Confronting them, you see no beginning.
Following them, you see no end.

Yet, riding the plowless plow
can seed the timeless Tao,
harvesting the secret
transcendence of the Now.

COMMENTARY

What is beyond sight, hearing and touching —
even beyond reason and experience? A world
without the rising light or the setting darkness,
where there is neither form nor image, neither
beginning nor end.

It is the elusive indefinable and paradoxical
Great Integrity of the universe, the Tao, which
transcends time, space and matter.

What use for the Great Integrity do we human
beings have when we are absorbed in acquiring
ten thousand[12] possessions? None. Even worse, it
subverts our false values, premises, goals and
institutions. The Great Integrity is an invitation
to the most radical transformation of our lives
and consciousness. It is a challenge to transcend
civilization as fragmentation and acquisitiveness,
an open door to re-enter life with an
uncompromised humanity, totally synergistic
with the universe.

Because it is subversive, the Great Integrity
appears in disguise, as a secret transcendence.

In ancient times
the people knew the Great Integrity
with subtlety and profundity.

Because they are so unfathomable to us,
we can describe the ancients
only with great effort.

They were –
cautious as those crossing an icy stream,
wary as those surrounded by dangers,
dignified as guests,
yielding as melting ice,
innocent as virgin wood,
open and broad as valleys,
merging freely as muddy water.

But today, who can remain patient
while the mud so gradually clears?
Who can remain still
while the moment for action
so slowly emerges?

Who?
We observers of the Great Integrity,
who in our times,
like those ancients,
never seeking fulfillment,
are never unfulfilled.

COMMENTARY

Ancient times for us twenty-first century readers of the *Tao Te Ching* represents a *double entendre*. We can stand back with Lao Tzu, living in the sixth century BCE and view his ancient times, by which he means tribal times, and perhaps also the first one thousand years of Chinese civilization, that is, around six thousand to five thousand years ago during the era of the three first legendary emperors. We can also stand back from our own twenty-first century. Then, ancient times for us are Lao Tzu's own time. Lao Tzu says that the ancients lived so long ago that they are unfathomable and can be described only with great effort. For us today, the task is two and a half millennia more formidable. Like Lao Tzu, when I speak to my contemporaries of the Great Integrity, they laugh.[13] They say people have never been like that. They have always been selfish and competitive. What they mean, of course, is that this is the way people have been throughout our recorded history, which for us westerners is about three thousand years, that is, since ancient Greece emerged from its tribal beginnings, and only a few hundred years before the time of Lao Tzu. So the seven metaphors of the third stanza of this verse are, in some ways, even more unfathomable for us than for Lao Tzu's contemporaries because we are so much more removed from those in tribal times who experienced the Great Integrity.

On the other hand, there are two ways that we twenty-first century-ites have become more capable of understanding the Great Integrity than any previous generation living in civilizations:

1) Some of us have become familiar with modern anthropological studies of tribal peoples who lived the Great Integrity, and 2) Some of us have begun to be aware that twenty-first century technology can open the door to a new planetary economic abundance. When this awareness is coupled with a new global consciousness, we begin to visualize the Great Integrity as the core of our immediate personal and social agendas.

The fourth stanza returns us to a time contemporary with the writing of the *Tao Te Ching* expressing the impatience that the people then had in acquiring a Tao consciousness and way of life. Lao Tzu asks, *who can remain patient while the mud so gradually clears? Who can remain still while the moment for action so slowly emerges?*

For those of us reading it today, this impatience is even greater since it is our generations, not Lao Tzu's, who have the potential to live the Great Integrity. However, the closer we come to grasping the Great Integrity, the more elusive it seems to become, since the patterns of the past cling ever more desperately, the nearer we come to replacing them.

Allow the heart to empty itself of all turmoil!
Retrieve the utter tranquillity of mind
from which you issued.

Although all forms are dynamic,
and we all grow and transform,
each of us is compelled to return to our root.
Our root is quietude.

To fully return to our root
    is to be enlightened.
Never to experience tranquillity
    is to act blindly,
a sure path to disaster.

To know tranquillity is to embrace all.
To embrace all is to be just.
Justice is the foundation for wholeness.
Wholeness is the Great Integrity.
The Great Integrity
    is the infinite fulfilling itself.

COMMENTARY

Ever since we human beings acquired the capacity to feel separate from all that is *Not-I*, a process sociologists call *alienation*, we have lost the tranquillity that is inherent in living as an inextricable part of nature. This process escalated during the evolution of what we euphemistically call *civilization*, the predominant form of society during these past few millennia. In civilizations, we not only became *separated* from all that is *Not-I*, but we became the *enemies* of each other, of our environment, and even of ourselves. Consequently, we have had to invent cultural compensations for our loss of wholeness and for our destructive social relations. Religion (holiness) and the arts (creativity) were developed as virtual institutions that help us to momentarily re-experience the harmony and tranquillity that is no longer inherent in everyday life.

Here Lao Tzu reminds us that it is the nature of nature to emerge from and return to the peace of undifferentiated oneness, that is, to the Great Integrity, and the failure to do so is fatal.

There are four types of leaders:
The best leader
    is indistinguishable from the will
    of those who selected her.
The next best leader
    enjoys the love and praise of the people.
The poor leader
    rules through coercion and fear.
And the worst leader
    is a tyrant despised by the multitudes
    who are the victims of his power.

What a world of difference
    among these leaders!
In the last two types,
    what is done is without sincerity or trust –
    only coercion.
In the second type,
    there is a harmony
    between the leader and the people.
In the first type,
    whatever is done happens so naturally
    that no one presumes to take the credit!

COMMENTARY

We are familiar with all these kinds of leaders except for the first type. In the early days of their revolutions, Thomas Jefferson, Vladimir Lenin, Mao Tse-Tung and Fidel Castro were the second type. Josef Stalin ruled through coercion and fear. And Hitler was certainly a tyrant who was despised by hundreds of millions of people throughout the world.

Those leaders who rule by fear, coercion and tyranny do not acquire and sustain their power simply by some mysterious force. Such leaders require an army of people who are willing to serve as enforcers of injustice. Furthermore, and what may at first consideration be astonishing, often such leaders first come to power through at least the tacit approval of the majority, even though it leads to their victimization. How can such irrationality envelop an entire nation like a plague?[14] Some answers are suggested by Lao Tzu in the next three verses (18, 19 and 20), which elucidate some of the consequences of losing the Great Integrity.

Where do we find examples of the first type of leaders – the kind whose leadership is so indistinguishable from the will of those who select them that no one presumes to take the credit for anything that is done? Indeed, such leaders are not to be found anywhere in the written history of civilizations. Only pre-civilization leaders in democratic and egalitarian tribal societies had no need, nor possibility to take credit for the interactive cooperative efforts and accomplishments of the entire community.[15]

In Lao Tzu's time there was no way that such a totally democratic community could re-emerge. That is possible only today now that we have a technology that can provide the material and cultural needs of all people on our planet. For us to continue to make war with each other, and to continue to elect leaders who carry out inhuman sectarian acts, is now a social insanity. How much more clearly, then, do Lao Tzu's insights enlighten *our* thinking today and clarify *our* alternatives than those of his contemporaries or those of any other generations before or after the sixth century BCE!

Verse

18 THE PARADOXES OF ABANDONING THE GREAT INTEGRITY

When the Great Integrity was abandoned,
humanity and justice appeared.

When knowledge and teachers appeared,
hypocrisy was their inevitable accompaniment.

When family relationships lost their harmony,
filial piety and parental affection
were suddenly birthed.

When a nation succumbs to chaos
and corruption,
patriotic politicians are always at hand
announcing themselves.

COMMENTARY

When civilization exchanged the Great Integrity for the universal fragmentation of all entities, integrity was sacrificed at the altar of measuring and pricing each fragment.

This process of integrity dismemberment is rationalized by logical ideologies, which are intellectualizations that are severed from holistic life experience. Accordingly, Lao Tzu ignores these vested static logical illusions, preferring to speak in the paradoxical language of processes and transformations.

In this verse, it is implied that many people celebrate "humanity" and "justice" as ideal universal virtues. But Lao Tzu knows that when the Great Integrity was abandoned, *inhumanity* and *injustice* became universal experiences. He also reminds us that we have come to know humanity only as a release from the inhumanity that dominates life.

In fact, there can be no awareness of humanity without inhumanity, no justice without injustice, right without wrong. As *Verse 2 — Relativity* points out, we know beauty because there is ugly and good because there is evil. The Great Integrity does not know justice because it does not know injustice.

This verse thereby implies part of the answer to the question in the previous *Verse 17 — Leaders:* Why should a majority contribute to their own victimization? One way is by succumbing to the ideologies that rationalize inequities and injustices as though they are inherent in life itself rather than the consequences of selling our holistic souls (the Great Integrity) to the fragmentized market place. By accepting these ideologies as universal truths, we accommodate to our own shackles.

19 THE PARADOXES OF RETURNING TO THE GREAT INTEGRITY

Banish the intellectual!
Discard knowledge!
We will all benefit a hundredfold!

Eliminate all institutions of charity
    and justice!
We can then return
to our natural love for each other.

Let everyone be released
from our addictions to shrewdness and profit!
Then, thievery will disappear!

These three negate the Great Integrity.
But to negate these negations is insufficient.
Three affirmations are also necessary.

The first is to embrace simplicity and integrity.
The second is to consume
    only the needs of our body and soul.
The third is to allow our love and concern
    for others to define our essentiality.

COMMENTARY

Lao Tzu suggests that we discard knowledge and eliminate charity and justice. He doesn't ask us to discard ignorance and eliminate selfishness and injustice as we might expect from someone who is dedicated to improving life. There are two implications in Lao Tzu's carefully selected terminology:

(1) For Lao Tzu, it is not enough only to *reduce* ignorance, selfishness and injustice. These despicable characteristics need to be entirely eliminated. When ignorance no longer exists, there cannot be intellectuals who are the only knowledgeable ones. When no one is deprived, charity will have no use and will disappear from our lives and vocabularies. When injustice disappears, the concept of justice will have no meaning.

But during the time of Lao Tzu in the sixth century BCE and right up to our own time, the elimination of poverty, ignorance, selfishness and injustice has been only a utopian dream. However, today, for the first time in history, our new incredible technologies have created the possibility of fulfilling everyone's needs on the planet. In this sense, Lao Tzu was born more than two and a half millennia before his time. It is only now that we are able not only to appreciate, but also to fulfill, his vision of a life in harmony with itself. This is why people of his own time were relatively deaf to Lao Tzu, the impractical rebel. Now, in this twenty-first century, unless we transform our way of life and our consciousness in the radical ways suggested by Lao Tzu, we are all likely to become our own omnicidal victims while screaming to the very end, like Voltaire's *Candide*, that we live in the best of all possible worlds.

(2) In a world in which ideologies function as rationales for inequities, logic can be utilized manipulatively. Lao Tzu's frequent use of paradox *(Discard knowledge and we will all benefit a hundredfold!)* is a way of shocking us and shaking up our old modes of thinking so that we become open to an alternative consciousness. For us, it is also an in-your-face rejection of Platonian and Cartesian logic as rigid, mechanistic and anachronistic.

This verse not only points out the obstacles to our experiencing life holistically, it also declares three prerequisites: 1) to embrace simplicity and integrity, 2) to consume only the needs of our body and soul, and 3) to allow our love and concern for others (and, of course, for ourselves) to define our identities.

Verse 20

THE SADNESS OF SUPERFICIALITIES AND OF THE UNFULFILLED GREAT INTEGRITY

It is sometimes deeply depressing to be a rebel,
knowing that we can never share
    most people's way of life,
nor can they share ours.

Schooling stuffs the brains of our children
    with trivia.
The more the trivia, the more their anxieties.
They indoctrinate the children
to believe that the consequences are grave
when they fail to distinguish "good" from "evil",
and agreement from disagreement.
What gross nonsense!

To escape the rubbish
of all this so-called knowledge,
in the winter, people run
to the great feasts of lamb, pork and ox,
and they climb high in the mountains
to view the first signs of spring.

We are so different!
Having no desire for the trivialities,
nor for their compensations,
We are like infants not yet knowing
    how to laugh!
Ever wandering, and having no home
    to which we may return.

While most people are obsessed
    with superficialities,
we feel empty.
While most people feel they know so much,
we feel simple-minded.
While most people believe they live happily
in the best of all possible worlds,
we are despaired to witness this world!

It is so painful to know
    that we will always be outsiders,
endlessly moving like the ocean,
aimlessly blowing like the wind.

While we fear what others fear,
we don't treasure what others treasure.
Our treasure is the Great Integrity.
However, until it is shared,
it will not be the Universal Integrity,
for we are part of them,
    and they are part of us.

194

COMMENTARY

How often we who are rebels have despaired! We identify with Lao Tzu and his frustrations. We have so often shared his sadness and his discouragement of not being accepted by either the power elite or by the majority who are often cleverly manipulated to identify with the very views that victimize them.

Of course, those who have the power and the privileges of wealth are opposed to any radical changes. They want to conserve their power and privileges, so they are known as conservatives, though some pretend to side with the people, giving themselves liberal sounding names.

The privileged elite also controls the main belief systems that rationalize the inequities of power. Today, they do so by owning and controlling the main media that mold the views of the public. Even more fundamentally, they control the jobs that provide the money that buys all the necessities of life. No wonder we have a hard time being heard! No wonder we feel isolated and alienated from the main streams of social, political and economic life!

Such have been the frustrations of us rebels since the time of Lao Tzu. But, at last, today we have an alternative. We can form a global community and return to the Great Integrity when children will no longer be indoctrinated with trivia, and adults will no longer suffer the inhumanities that are masked by overindulgent escapes. It makes us wish that Lao Tzu were among us to appreciate and celebrate these new opportunities. But, of course, he is – in these very verses!

Verse
21 THE GREAT INTEGRITY IS A PARADOX

The Great Integrity is a paradox.
It is inherent in the universe,
yet its form is so illusive.
It is the Vital Essence of every entity,
yet nothing announces its essential character.

The Great Integrity was apparent
before time, space and matter
    appeared to separate.
How can we re-mind and re-infuse ourselves
with this very touchstone
    of all essentialities and connections?

By re-fusing time, space and matter
with the spiritualization of our materiality,
and with the materialization
    of our spirituality.

Then, when our dualities and numeralities
    become blurred and forgotten,
the Great Integrity will re-emerge in forms
of such incredible depths and dimensions
    of enlightenment
precisely because our temporary
    fragmentary consciousness
created a multi-millennial amnesia.

COMMENTARY

In this case, I took some liberties with the translation to bring Lao Tzu's essential idea of the Great Integrity as paradox into contemporary terms and issues. While Lao Tzu refers to substance, essence, and belief and the fragmentation of all things and ideas, I translate this as the separation of time, space and matter. Of course, the integrity of energy, time, space and matter which Lao Tzu intuits and calls the Great Integrity has been scientifically verified by Einstein, with its specific relations defined by his well-known $e = mc^2$ equation.

Even by Lao Tzu's time, dualism and quantifications began to replace the Great Integrity in the categorizing and enumerating of the "ten thousand things". Of course, modern institutions and science since the time of Descartes and Newton greatly escalated the process. Gradually, competition and fragmentation began more and more to appear as the nature of nature and of the universe, thereby rationalizing the organization of societies into competing units as natural and inevitable. The accompanying philosophies dichotomized mind and matter, spirituality and materiality, and provided the ideological basis for the separation of religion from science. Each philosophy and religion developed its own explanation for how misery and inhumanity are inherent in the nature of everything that doesn't reside in heaven.

But it was this very fragmentized consciousness that produced modern science and technology, which, in turn, now provides the material basis for the possibility for planetary abundance. As we approach the establishment of a possible egalitarian planetary community, the dualistic underpinnings of life as relative scarcity can begin to crumble, allowing us to spiritualize our materiality and materialize our spirituality.

We are poised to set foot on the social and personal paths toward re-achieving the Great Integrity which Lao Tzu's contemporaries could realize only in their meditations and dreams. Here's to the multi-millennial period of Great Integrity amnesia, which paradoxically was our historical prerequisite to re-achieving the Great Integrity itself on a higher level than nature first expressed it. Before human beings, the Great Integrity was the unconscious common experience of all life. Now we human beings can re-create it and live it consciously, a unique capability of our species.

22 CELEBRATE PARADOX!

No-thing remains itself.
Each prepares the path to its opposite.

To be ready for wholeness, first be fragmented.
To be ready for rightness, first be wronged.
To be ready for fullness, first be empty.
To be ready for renewal, first be worn out.
To be ready for success, first fail.
To be ready for doubt, first be certain.

Because the wise observe the world through
    the Great Integrity,
they know they are not knowledgeable.
Because they do not perceive
    only through their perceptions,
they do not judge this right and that wrong.
Because they do not delight in boasting,
    they are appreciated.
Because they do not announce
    their superiority,
they are acclaimed.
Because they never compete,
no one can compete with them.

Verily, fragmentation prepares the path
    to wholeness,
the mother of all origins and realizations.

COMMENTARY

This verse is an elaboration on paradox of the previous four verses.[16] It seems that now we might be able to recover the Great Integrity precisely and paradoxically because we have suffered for so many centuries as victims of its loss.

Paradox and the transformation of any entity into its opposite is not only the nature of the Great Integrity, but of its own rebirth, and indeed, of all natural processes.

Verse

23   SINCERITY

Speak few words, but say them
    with quietude and sincerity,
and they will be long lasting,
for a raging wind cannot blow all morning,
nor a sudden rainstorm
    last throughout the day.

Why is this so?
Because it is the nature of the sky
    and the earth to be frugal.
Even human beings cannot alter this nature
without suffering the consequences.

When we sincerely follow the ethical path,
we become one with it.
When we become one with the ethical path,
it embraces us.

When we completely lose our way,
we become one with loss.
When we become one with loss,
loss embraces us.

When we sincerely follow the Great Integrity,
we become one with it.
When we are one with the Great Integrity,
it embraces us.

But when nothing is done sincerely,
no-thing and no one embraces us.

COMMENTARY

The actions of a sincere person speak for themselves. But when there is a contradiction between words and deeds, the space between them needs to be filled with mountains of rationalizations. Therefore, those who are sincere speak few words. Those who speak loquaciously are not sincere.

Very simply put, the Great Integrity and insincerity are as incompatible as honesty and dishonesty. When we choose insincerity and dishonesty there is always a price that we pay: to be left lonely and 'unembraced' in our exile from the Great Integrity.

Verse 24 AVOIDING VOIDS

Standing on tiptoe
    will only make you tipsy,
Walking with long strides
    will not allow a long walk.
Shining the light on yourself
    will never enlighten you.
Being self-righteous
    precludes you from being right.
Boasting about yourself
    will never boost your eminence.
Parading yourself
    parodies leadership.

Tao consciousness avoids
the cultivation of all these ego bloated voids.

COMMENTARY

All our artificialities, superficialities, and needs for parading our egos are compensations for the Great Void that derives from living loveless lives.

When this void will be transcended, our individual rhythms and goals will become coincident with our ecologies. This is what Lao Tzu means by the return of the Great Integrity when self and social actualizations will fill all the ego-bloated voids, releasing us from the compensatory addictions that we now so desperately cultivate.

Verse 25 NAMING THE NAMELESS

What preceded life?
The earth.
What preceded the earth?
The universe.
What preceded the universe?
The soundless and shapeless
origin of origins,
ever transforming
    and having no beginning nor end.

This Mother of the universe
is boundless, and nameless.
But if we wanted to share with you
anything about this remarkable
    non-executing executor,
we must invent a name for it.

We will call it the Tao
because Tao means great.[17]
Incredibly great
    because it occupies infinite space,
being fully present in the whole universe,
and in every infinitesimal particle.

Because this Great Integrity
    created the universe,
And the universe created the earth,
And the earth created us.
we are all incredibly great.

Life derives
    from the nature of the earth.
The earth derives
    from the nature of the universe.
The universe derives
    from the nature of the Great Integrity.
And the Great Integrity
    is the omnipresent, omnigenous omniform,
the universal material and spiritual substance,
and the holoversal interlinkage
    and coition of existence.[18]

25 NAMING THE NAMELESS

COMMENTARY

Here in this remarkable verse, we find Lao Tzu occupying (though never smugly) a more advanced scientific position than the most advanced science of the twenty-first century!

Certainly, physics, in both relativity and quantum theory, represents the most comprehensive analysis of the nature of the universe we live in compared with any of the other sciences. However, in macrophysics (relativity theory), even Einstein's $e=mc^2$, which demonstrated the inextricable relation of energy, matter and the speed of light, has not allowed physicists to go the full way with Lao Tzu who concluded 2700 years ago that there was never a beginning of time, matter, or space, and that the Great Integrity is infinite. Physicists, still search for the "beginning" of the universe, and now posit the "Big Bang" theory in their seemingly obstinate clinging to the last vestige of the particularistic Newtonian-Cartesian paradigm.

In twenty-first century microphysics (quantum theory), the search for the Holy Grail – the smallest particle of matter – has also still not been abandoned. Once thought to be the mighty atom, quantum physics has further reduced the fundamental fragment of the universe first to electrons, positrons and neutrons, then to neutrinos and antineutrinos, then further to photons, hadrons, quarks, antiquarks and mesons. Finally, quantum physics has posited that the particles themselves are not the most irreducible fragment of matter, but that even smaller components can be discerned as waves, specifically, as *superstrings*.

What indeed may very well become the most advanced scientific understanding of the nature of the universe is Lao Tzu's proposal of the Great Integrity where both the macro and the micro aspects meet in an irreducible infinitude without beginnings, endings or entities of any kind that are not related and interlinked. Indeed, physicist David Bohm's *holoverse* may be the conceptualization most closely related to Lao Tzu's *Great Integrity*, and to the reality of our universe whose integrity we seem to need to deny as long as part of us is at war with any other part. What Lao Tzu and David Bohm are suggesting is that the concept that we, and the universe we live in, are composed of discrete and separate parts is an illusion. Bohms definition of the holoverse is summarized below.

"Ultimately, the entire universe (with all its particles, including those constituting human beings, their laboratories, observing instruments, etc.) has to be understood as a single undivided whole, in which analysis into separately and independently existent parts has no fundamental status".[19]

Verse 26 SEDUCTIONS

Inner strength is the master
of all frivolities.
Tranquillity is the master
of all agitated emotions.

Those who succumb to frivolities
have lost their inner strength.
Those who succumb to agitated emotions
have lost their tranquillity.

The wise cultivate
inner strength and tranquillity.
That is why they are not seduced
by addictive temptations.

COMMENTARY

Living in a world before we have achieved the Great Integrity often challenges our inner strength and tranquillity, tempting us to give up these anchors to our human essence for addictive escapes from the stresses we are so frequently forced to confront.

We are reminded here that if we can embrace our inner strength and tranquillity when they are threatened by out-of-control addictions and emotions, we will stay the course toward the Great Integrity, and be grateful for having done so.

However, Lao Tzu invites no judgmental guilt or blame against those who don't hold fast, and for whatever reasons, let their addictions and runaway emotions hold sway at any moment. What on the surface here appears like a tautology is rather a profound insight that to feel guilt or blame for losing one's way to the Great Integrity are themselves emotional toxins that can only more deeply enmesh us in our victimizations.

27 WISDOM IS EFFORTLESS MUTUALITY

The expert traveler
leaves no footprints.
The expert speaker
makes no mispronunciations.
The expert in calculation
needs no calculator.

The expert in closing things
needs no lock,
yet not one can open
what has been closed.
The expert in binding
uses no knots,
yet no one can pull apart
what has been bound.

The expert in caring for things
never wastes anything.
The expert at helping people
never abandons anyone.

These are the paths to enlightenment.
Those who arrive at their destination
teach those who are still on the path,
while those still on the path
are sources of wisdom for the teachers.

COMMENTARY

We are reminded here that sharing wisdom requires two basic qualities: 1) an enlightened expertise and 2) an effortless mutuality.

No matter how good a traveler you may be, if you do it under stress, you will indeed leave evidence of your dis-ease. No matter how good a speaker you are, if there is a lack of agreement between you and your audience, you are likely to become inarticulate. No matter how good you are at counting, if you are counting something in which the others involved have an opposite vested interest, you are likely to make mistakes.

The wise who achieve an enlightened expertise in effortless mutuality teach those who are still on the path, but are always enriching themselves by learning from their students.

Verse 28   THE FUSION OF OPPOSITES

To know the masculine
 and be true to the feminine
is to be the waterway of the world.

To be the waterway of the world
is to flow with the Great Integrity,
always swirling back
     to the innocence of childhood.

To know yang and to be true to yin
is to echo the universe.

To echo the universe
is to merge with the Great Integrity,
ever returning to the infinite.

To know praise and be true to the lowly
is to be a model for the planet.

To be a model for the planet
 is to express the Great Integrity
as the Primal Simplicity –
     like an uncarved block.

When the uncarved block
goes to the craftsman,
it is transformed into something useful.

The wise craftsman
cuts as little as necessary
because he follows the Great Integrity.

COMMENTARY

First, we are reminded that all "ten-thousand things" of the universe are composed of opposites: masculine and feminine, yang and yin, high and low.

Second, Lao Tzu tells us that we should allow yin to be the dominant of the two opposites; that is, to know the masculine, but be true to the feminine, to know yang but be true to yin, to know praise but be true to the lowly.

Third, Lao Tzu observes that to merge with the Great Integrity is to ever return to the innocence of childhood, to the infinite, and to make useful things by minimal transformations of nature.

Yin predominated during the Neolithic era of communal matriarchal tribes. Our own age turned all this upside down.[20] Throughout recorded history, our civilizations have been male dominated, competitive, nature-destructive, and ruled by those who were the most aggressive and war-like. This is precisely why Lao Tzu finds it necessary to remind us that we have been living in opposition to nature, and that we need to return to the Great Integrity. How much more critical it is for us today to understand and to follow Lao Tzu's advice. Not to follow it in his time led to great unhappiness. Not to follow it in our time could lead to the end of our species on this planet.

Those who have most power and wealth
treat the planet as a thing to be possessed,
to be used and abused
    according to their own dictates.
But the planet is a living organism,
a Great Spiritual Integrity.

To violate this Integrity
is certain to cull forth disaster
since each and every one of us
is an inherent part
of this very organism.

All attempts to control the world
can only lead to its decimation
and to our own demise
since we are an inseparable part
of what we are senselessly trying to coerce.

Any attempt to possess the world
can only lead to its loss
and to our own dissolution
since we are an intrinsic part
of what we are foolishly trying to possess.

The world's pulse is our pulse.
The world's rhythms are our rhythms.
To treat our planet
    with care, moderation and love
is to be in synchrony with ourselves
and to live in the Great Integrity.

COMMENTARY

No other species on our planet has the capability of creating the three illusions that we civilized human beings cultivate.

The *first* illusion is that we are separate from the world in which we live.

The *second* is that this world we live in is there for us to use and abuse according to our arbitrary wishes. We are the only arrogant species.

This arrogance was born out of a *third* illusion — that each of us is naturally in competition with other members of our own species. This illusion allows us to accept the institutionalization of the principle that most of us are here on this planet to serve those who establish hegemony over us.

Lao Tzu questions these three premises, and postulates that they are corruptions and violations of the nature of nature which is rooted in the very opposite paradigm that he calls the Great Integrity. In Lao Tzu's Great Integrity we are all inherently inseparable from our environment and from each other.

Today his assumptions are convincing. Basically, the only reason that the people of Lao Tzu's time did not, and could not, follow his more humane premises is that the technology was not yet present that had the potential to fulfill his egalitarian principles.

Lao Tzu's teaching was subversive to the rationalizations of the three illusions. Perhaps this was one of the reasons he never wrote down his thoughts until he left civilization to spend the rest of his life secluded in the mountains. Even so, Lao Tzu's teachings must have begun to have had some impact as the country was undergoing a great escalation of corruption and inner power struggle.[21]

The economic limitations that generated the three illusions have now disappeared in this twenty-first century, making it possible for us to announce Lao Tzu's Great Integrity as a practical goal for our time. If this is unacceptable to those who control the planet's wealth, perhaps it is their time to go to the mountains.

30 DEFENSE AND AGGRESSION

Those on the path of the Great Integrity
never use military force to conquer others.
Every aggressive act
harvests its own counter-terrorism.

Wherever the military marches,
the killing fields lay waste to the land,
yielding years of famine and misery.

When attacked, those on the path
of the Great Integrity
defend themselves benevolently,
never revenging.

Achieve success without arrogance,
without seeking glory,
and without violating others.

Aggression leaches our strength
and humanity,
subverting the Great Integrity,
and inviting disaster.

COMMENTARY

Again and again Lao Tzu denounces military aggression. However, he is not a pacifist. While justifying defense against aggression, he warns against acquiring the character of the aggressor. He cautions to engage in defense benevolently, never revenging nor violating others, never seeking glory nor acting arrogantly.[22] Lastly, he reminds us that aggression leaches our strength and humanity, subverting the Great Integrity, and ultimately inviting disaster.

Of course, we twenty-first century-ites, being "blessed" with the ultimate nuclear, biological and chemical weapons, invite the ultimate disasters. Can we instead, embrace Lao Tzu's Great Integrity, and never again use military force to conquer others? For all of us, the answer to this question translates into the ultimate social choice: to be or not to be.

Verse
31 WAR

The finest weapons are the worst evils.
They are universally loathed.
Therefore, help guide your nation
    to the non-aggressive path.

The wise hold steady on the passive yin path.
Those who are aggressive
    prefer the active yang.

Weapons are instruments of coercion
    and devils of death.
Resort to them only in dire necessity.
Peace is our natural state of being.

If weapons must be wielded
    to defend ourselves,
and we are victorious, never rejoice.
Can there be joy over the slaughter of others?

On joyous occasions,
we attune with the yang side.
On sad occasions, with the yin.

During battle,
    the soldiers are on the left yang side,
engaging in the combat.
The commanders are on the right yin side,
observing the action.

After the battle,
    the soldiers who have slain others,
move to the yin side and mourn,
while the commanders,
    now on the yang side,
are celebrating victory
    even though it is a funeral.

31 WAR

COMMENTARY

Clearly, Lao Tzu stands opposed to war and all forms of aggression, but he condones defending oneself when attacked. However, even in the midst of self-defense, he calls for a consciousness that the use of weapons, the worst of all evils, is always a violation of our natural state of peacefulness. Furthermore, when we are victorious in defending ourselves from aggressors, this is no cause for rejoicing because we have violated our own humanity by killing others.

In Chinese medicine and philosophy the left side of the body is the yang or more active side while the right side is the yin or more nurturing side. The Chinese doctor palpates both the left and right radial arteries in different positions and depths as an important method of diagnosis. When a patient is healthy, it is normal for the left yang side to be a little stronger. Western medicine also observes the same differentiation, pointing out that the heart which pumps blood to all our arteries is located more on the left side of the chest cavity.

More recent observations of brain function[23] differentiate the left side of the cerebral cortex as being more language and logic oriented, and so more capable of serving reasoning as well as rationalizing and manipulating roles. The right side of the cerebral cortex is identified as serving more intuitive, sensual and passive functions. Therefore, in Chinese terms, the left side of the brain is functionally more yang and the right side more yin. We are further

reminded that there are some emotions that are more active and therefore relatively yang, such as celebrating joyous occasions, while other emotions are more passive and therefore more yin, such as sadness and grief.

Lao Tzu observes that during the battle, the soldier functions in a more yang way because he is the one engaging in combat. Therefore, he is metaphorically on the left yang side. On the other hand, the commanders, who are more likely to give the orders and stand back from the action, are thereby serving a more yin function. They are metaphorically on the right side.

Lastly, he provides the final paradoxical insight, observing that after the battle, their respective roles reverse. The soldiers, who have slain others, grieve for those whom they killed, thereby expressing their yin side, that is, their sadness. On the contrary, the commanders, who usually reap the credit for the victory, are prone to celebrate and be filled with their own ego satisfactions, a more yang expression.

Verse
32
IS IT NOT TIME TO UNIFY THE FRAGMENTS?

Although the Great Integrity is infinite,
and therefore undefined,
it is silent in its Primal Simplicity.

Nothing is its superior.
When humanity embraces the Great Integrity,
all life on earth will be grateful.

All yin and yang will be harmonized
*   in the sweet daily dew,*
and peace will reign on the planet
without anyone commanding it.

When the Primal Simplicity atomized
*   into the 10,000 fragments,*
with their 10,000 names,
our planet became endangered.

Now – are there not enough fragments?
Is it not time to stop and return
*   to the universal sea*
from which all streams emerged?

To return to the Great Integrity
is to obliterate
the list of the 10,000 endangered species.

COMMENTARY

In one sense, the ability to separate self from the environment began when our species became self-conscious. No other species on the planet has the ability to be aware of its own existence.

This estrangement took a qualitative leap when communal tribal life gave way to civilizations, which pitted individuals and groups within society against each other. Thus the loss of the Great Integrity began in China about five thousand years ago, and Lao Tzu, who is said to have lived during the sixth century BCE, was already the product of more than two thousand years of fragmentation.

A third and higher level of fragmentation took place in modern times and led to the objectification expressed by the new mathematics of René Descartes, the new science of Isaac Newton, and the new form of human relations that looked on working people as a cost of production. This level was never experienced by Lao Tzu, but has been all too familiar to our generations of the past few hundred years.

Ten thousand is the number that the ancient Chinese used to signify the endless quantifications that all civilizations generate. Lao Tzu asks here, is it not time to stop fragmenting and return to our reunification with the universe represented by the Great Integrity? Although the loss of the Great Integrity in Lao Tzu's time threatened everyone's well being, it is not until our day that it has resulted in the extinction of thousands of species, and now also places our own species on the endangered list. My translation updates his question, placing it in the context of the new mega-madnesses of genocide, speciescide and even omnicide.[24]

In Lao Tzu's time, the possibility of returning to the Great Integrity, that is, to a holistic life style and consciousness, was not realizable except spiritually, and even on this level it was attainable only by a few intellectuals like Lao Tzu whose full bellies, advanced consciousness, and relative independence, permitted what we might call a pseudo-holism. For the vast majority even pseudo-holism was an impossibility. As John Donne so succinctly pointed out, since no one is an island, entire by itself, when the bell tolls for one, it tolls for all. When liberation is not realizable by everyone, no one can completely return to the Great Integrity.

But today we are at that unique evolutionary stage when we can achieve an uncompromising integrity, when we can fulfill our human species capabilities, something that until now has been given to us only as a potential. Paradoxically, as Lao Tzu would point out if he were living today, we can now achieve the universal Great Integrity through those very ten thousand technologies that destroyed this integrity.

Verse 33 WHO ARE YOU?

If you understand others,
   you are astute.
If you understand yourself,
   you are insightful.

If you master others,
   you are uncommonly forceful.
If you master yourself,
   you have uncommon inner strength.

If you know when you have enough,
   you are wealthy.
If you carry your intentions to completion,
   you are resolute.

If you find your roots and nourish them,
   you will know longevity.
If you live a long creative life,
   you will leave an eternal legacy.

COMMENTARY

In this verse, each couplet implies a comparative hierarchy of fulfillment. It is more fulfilling to understand yourself than to understand others. It is more fulfilling to have inner strength than to be forceful. It is more fulfilling to carry your intentions to completion than to know when you've had enough. And it is more fulfilling, not only for you, but also for all future generations, to live a long creative life rather than just a long one.[25]

Verse
34 HUMILITY AND GREATNESS

The Great Integrity is unboundable
    like a flood.
It cannot be manipulated this or that way.
It is the very wellspring of life,
always outpouring, never commanding.

Although the source for every need,
it is never demanding.
It does its work silently
and unpretentiously.

All return to the Great Integrity
as our liberating universal home.
By never seeking greatness,
greatness permeates in deed.

COMMENTARY

In other verses, Lao Tzu reminds us that our "normal" lives are so coercive that living in harmony with the Great Integrity seems impossible. How difficult it is, for example, to imagine receiving the most bountiful gifts without demanding them, or doing our work without announcing our successes, or experiencing greatness without seeking it. But, according to Lao Tzu, and to most leaders of the new consciousness and alternative social relations movements of our own time, we can return to the Great Integrity as our liberating universal home, and when we do, such behaviors will become our normal experience.

When you merge with the universe,
the whole world is attracted to you,
discovering through you,
its own security, peace and good health.

Passing guests may stop by –
at first attracted to your savory food
*   and inspirational music.*
But they might leave more deeply enriched
than they could have anticipated –

Because the silent song of Tao
is the ultimate music,
and the infinite delicacy of Tao
is the consummate nourishment.

COMMENTARY

Lao Tzu is no dualistic ascetic who deprecates the body and worships the soul. He doesn't preach that the ultimate peace is found only after death (provided, of course, that you have obeyed the commandments of your particular sect). On the contrary, his guests are attracted by his excellent food and music. However, when they leave, they may not only be sensually and alimentally satiated, but they might also become introduced to the wondrous experience of merging with the universal Great Integrity.

Verse 36 TOO MUCH INVITES DISASTER

What is overexpanded becomes diminished.
What is too strong becomes weakened.
What is too high is cut down.
What is overpossessed becomes impoverished.

It is in the nature of process
     that in the final stages,
those who are overextended,
overarmed and overprivileged,
shall be overcome.

Disaster stalks the fish
which swims up from its deep water home,
and the army which threatens to conquer
those beyond its own borders.

COMMENTARY

My translation of this verse expresses what Lao Tzu could only imply. If he were as openly rebellious in his language as expressed in the translation, he might never have reached the more than ninety years he was supposed to have lived!

Specifically, while my last line cautions about armies being used to conquer others, Lao Tzu's words are more literally: *A nation's weapons should be shown to no one.*

Similarly, the metaphors Lao Tzu uses as arguments for his conclusion only imply the issue of overabundance and overprivilege. The more literal translation of his first lines is:

> If one wants to diminish, one must first expand.
> If one wants to weaken, one must first
>   strengthen.
> If one wants to cut something down,
>   it must first be promoted.
> If one wants to take something away,
>   it must first have been given.

However, as literally stated, the propositions do not conform to Lao Tzu's own premises. The process of diminishing does not necessarily follow any expansion, but requires overexpansion. The process of weakening does not necessarily follow strengthening but requires overstrengthening or overarming, and so forth. It is only the excess condition that produces its opposite. Therefore my translation not only is intended to clarify the conclusion that Lao Tzu (or his disciples) may not have dared to state blatantly, but also to more accurately express the metaphors upon which the conclusion is based.

Verse 37 THE PRIMAL SIMPLICITY

The Great Integrity imposes no action,
yet it leaves nothing undone.
Were governments to embrace it,
everything would develop naturally.

If thereafter an old ego should reincarnate,
the already permeated Primal Simplicity
would neutralize it in its pervasive silence.

Returning to silence is returning to peace.
Returning to peace,
    the world reharmonizes itself.

COMMENTARY

When the great transformation of our planet takes place, and we return to the Great Integrity, that doesn't mean that all the old habits will automatically disappear forever. It is likely that old egos will reincarnate for a while. However, once the new social condition permeates widely and deeply enough, we should expect that these old aberrations will tend to be more and more readily neutralized by a more and more widely and deeply pervading milieu of peace and harmony.

You can readily recognize
 the highest virtuousness
because it never places itself on display.
You can readily recognize
 the lowest virtuousness
because it is always announcing itself.

The highest virtue
 quietly serves universal needs.
The lowest virtue
 actively strives for personal success.
The highest morality serves common needs.
The lowest morality is self-serving.

True benevolence
acts without intention.
But when rituals go unheeded,
they are enforced with rolled-up sleeves.

Failing the Great Integrity,
 we resort to virtuousness.
Failing virtuousness,
 we resort to moralizing.
Failing moralizing, we resort to dogma,
the most superficial form
 of faith and loyalty,
and the nourishment for confusion.

Natural persons are attracted
to substance rather than form,
to the nutritious fruit
 rather than the enticing flower,
to that which dwells deeply within,
rather than to that which clings
 superficially to the surface.

COMMENTARY

The focus of this verse is on distinguishing the highest from the lowest forms of morality.

The highest forms of morality are directed to serving the needs of others, and are carried out quietly, with humility, naturally, and without self-conscious intention.

The lowest forms are precisely the opposite. They are motivated by ego satisfactions, fulfilling personal self-interests, and by announcing their own beneficence.

Four specific levels of integrity are differentiated from the highest level: the Great Integrity, to the lowest level: the coercive enforcement of dogma and ritual. In between is virtuousness and moralizing that are middle grounds between the highest and lowest moralities.

It is interesting to note that Lao Tzu had nothing but contempt for ritual, while for Confucius, his younger contemporary, ritual was the pinnacle of virtue. How ironic that, according to legend, Confucius went to visit Lao Tzu to become enlightened on matters of ritual since Lao Tzu held the position of archivist for the State of Chu. Needless to say, Confucius stormed out of his audience with Lao Tzu denouncing him as a dangerous dragon! Soon after this incident, it is said that Lao Tzu – only in mid-life – retired from his official position and fled to the mountains to live the rest of his life in seclusion.[26]

Verse
39 THEN AND NOW

In ancient times, all entities
    had their own integrity and function.
The sky was clear and endless.
The earth was calm and firm.
The gods were charged with spiritual powers.
The wells were clean and full.
The 10,000 creatures were healthy
    and fecund.
Leaders were elected to plan the work
    and defense of the community.
How wondrously concordant!

If the sky were not endless,
it could have fallen.
If the earth were not firm,
it could have burst.
If the gods did not exercise
    their spiritual powers,
they would have been abandoned.
If the wells were not full,
they could have dried up.
If the 10,000 creatures were not productive,
they could have become extinct.
If the leaders did not plan the work
    and defense of the community,
they would have been replaced.
In this way, each entity
    had its own essentiality,
each part complementing every other.

Nowadays, when the privileged among us
identify themselves with the orphan,
    the widower and the hungry one,
it may be an opportunistic appeal
    for the support of the lowly,
or a realization that loudly trumpeting
    self-glory negates itself,
or a premonition that shining like jade,
    and resounding like stone chimes
attracts the desperate adventurers
    among those deprived of hope,
inviting disaster among those
    who create these deprivations.

COMMENTARY

In ancient times, when all lived as part of the Great Integrity, each had its own function, performing it with integrity and with respect for all other entities. When one did not fulfill its function, it was replaced for the good of all, because poor functioning of one entity threatened all others.

Nowadays, (from even before the time of Lao Tzu right through our own day), the privileged tend to care only for their own well-being, while the under-privileged are deprived of realizing their capabilities and of benefiting from the bountifulness of all the available resources. The former, having for the most part lost their moral integrity, tend to rationalize these inequities in the ten thousand opportunistic masquerades, some of which Lao Tzu lists in the final stanza.

Verse

40 ALL IS PARADOX

The movement of the Great Integrity
is infinite,
yet its character is passive.
Being defines every form of life,
yet all originate in,
and return to, non-being.

COMMENTARY

The "Old Wise Man" never tires of reminding us that our senses and our logic are more illusion than reality. Wisdom, he says, derives rather from paradox, which in turn derives from the contradictions in our observations and conclusions, as well as from the very nature of transformation, which is itself, the defining character of the universe.

What is the nature of transformation? It is the tendency for everything when it becomes extreme to turn into its opposite. When we are overactive (extreme yang in Chinese terms) we must rest or sleep (yin) or else we will not survive. When we stay outside in very cold weather for a long time (extreme yin) we must find some source of heat (yang) or else we might die.

The main application of paradox and the principle of opposites for us today is that having reached the point in the development of modern civilization of extreme violence, competitiveness and fragmentation (extreme yang) we are now seeding the transformation to its opposite: Lao Tzu's Great Integrity (yin). Here is a key to our closet of lost hopes. Indeed, we have been appointed by evolution to become the conscious agents of our own transcendence.

Clearly, in order to accommodate us to continue to participate in a now anachronistic competitive ego-driven world of *haves* at war with the *have-nots*, we are asked to accept our social condition and its rationalizations as the only one possible and desirable in this "best of all possible worlds". (Voltaire) The spirit of Lao Tzu has reincarnated in his *Tao Te Ching* to invite us to laugh at these mythologies that serve only the selfish interests of the over-privileged. Lao Tzu keeps confronting us with an alternative consciousness that reminds us again and again that change, not permanence, is the nature of reality, and that the process of change is characterized by the yin-yang paradox. Thus, *the movement of the Great Integrity is infinite, yet its character is passive. Being defines every form of life, yet all originate in, and return to, non-being.*

41 OBSERVING AND NOURISHING PARADOX

When most people
        hear about the Great Integrity,
they waiver between belief and disbelief.
When wise people
        hear about the Great Integrity,
they diligently follow its path.
When ignorant people hear about it
they laugh out loud!
By this very laughter, we know its authenticity.

It is said that –
enlightenment appears dark,
the progressive way appears retrograde,
the smooth way appears jagged,
the highest peak of revelation
        appears empty like a valley,
the cleanest appears to be soiled,
the greatest abundance appears insufficient,
the most enduring inner strength
        appears like weakness,
and creativity appears imitative.

Great talents mature slowly.
Great sounds are silent.
Great forms look shapeless.
Transcendent squareness has no corners.

The Great Integrity hides behind all forms,
stubbornly nourishing
        the paradoxes that can enlighten us.

COMMENTARY

One of the important differentiations between the thought structures of Lao Tzu and of conventional science is the metaphoric-paradoxic character of the former and the objective and logical character of the latter. To Lao Tzu, contradictions often reveal a deep truth. To modern science, contradictions indicate an error. This verse is saturated with the paradoxes that surface when one experiences life through the Great Integrity, that is, through our intuitive holistic consciousness.

It is the left cerebral hemisphere[27] that formulates logical alienated thinking, which requires the modern conventional scientist to separate himself from that which he is investigating.

In contrast, the Great Integrity is a holistic consciousness, which predominantly activates the right cerebral hemisphere and is both phylogenetically and ontogenetically an earlier mode of perception.[28] Right brain dominance was characteristic of the first few million years that hominids wandered through our planet. It is also the only form of perception of every one of us during our infancy and the dominant form during our prelogical early childhood years.[29]

According to Lao Tzu and to many of us who are exploring a more appropriate consciousness for the twenty-first century, a new Great Integrity will transcend our present objective consciousness. My view of evolutionary transformation proposes that this new Great

Integrity will not be a return to right hemispheric dominance, but to a new left-right hemispheric merger in which both our thoughts and feelings, our objective apperceptions and subjective perceptions, will function as a higher level of integral human exchange. Such a development assumes a new mode of communication that will be objective and scientific (like language) as well as subjective and feelingful (like music), but without the duality that now characterizes their relationship. The new music-language might also permit the communication of simultaneous multiplicities, especially involving the processes of transformation. Until now, the limitations inherent in the linearity of our thinking and of our languages have required us to communicate the complexities of our experiences by analyzing and presenting them in sequential fragments like the frame-by-frame photographs in a cinema.

Verse 42   THE PRINCIPLES OF TRANSFORMATION

The Great Integrity expresses one.
One manifests as two.
Two is transformed into three.
And three generates all the myriad entities
    of the universe.

Every entity always returns to yin
after engaging yang.
The fusion of these two opposites
births the Vital Energy
    that sustains the harmony of life.

But for most people,
this harmony is decimated
by inheriting a condition
of relative misery, scarcity and victimization.

Politicians cleverly pretend
    that they too originate
from the toxic soil of this misery,
even while designing the very laws
that legitimate victimization.

But watch out –
    those who hoard oversufficiency
will be diminished!
And those who are diminished
will become bountiful!

These commonly known truths
that common people
teach each other,
are also my truths.

As you sow,
so shall you reap.
Such is the heart of my teaching
in a world forced to live heartlessly.

COMMENTARY

This verse summarizes the origin and theory of the Great Integrity (*Tao*) its practice (*Te*), its violations, and the teachings that can function as guides (*Ching*) to return us to a holistic and integral life (*Tao*). The evolution of the Great Integrity is summarized in the first short stanza which encapsulates the intuitive wisdom of the ancients, and which is now validated by the latest scientific theories.

Specifically, this evolution is postulated as being rooted in the great underlining truth of the universe as expressing the metaphor of *one*. We can now in the twenty-first century translate that metaphor as a recognition that every entity in the universe is related to and inherent in every other part. In the early 1970s, I discovered that the ancient Chinese Vital Energy (Qi or Ch'i) system of acupoints and channels is reiterated in each part of the body, and furthermore, that each of these anatomical parts manifests acupoints to the rest of the body that are hologrammatic to the anatomy of the body.[30] I called these *micro-acupuncture systems*. Karl Pribram discovered that the brain was also holonomic, and that each part of the brain, contained the knowledge of the whole brain.[31] Microbiologists have discovered that "in every single cell of every human organism, the sum total of the whole life experience of every living organism since the beginning of time is preserved".[32] David Bohm, a colleague of Albert Einstein, applied the holonomic concept to the nature of the entire universe.[33] All of these investigations translate Lao Tzu's intuitive concept of the Great Integrity in scientific terms.[34]

The Great Integrity manifests as *two* through the universality of opposites: passive and active, cold and hot, wet and dry, slow and fast, low and high, slow and fast, negative and positive – all of which are categorized by the ancient Chinese as yin and yang.

Since the time of Hegel (1770-1831), modern dialectics has shown how the *two* is transformed into *three*. Hegel reveals how everything in the universe is always involved in transformation, and that every process involves the conflict of opposites (yin and yang, thesis and antithesis), which resolves into a third entity (synthesis).[35]

This verse also reminds us how the Great Integrity has been violated by human beings, in civilizations, who disturb the natural harmony that nature continually re-establishes in its transformational processes. Lastly, Lao Tzu tells us that it is the common truths that common people teach each other, which are also his truths, through which we will return once again to the Great Integrity and end our heartless way of life.

43 THE VALUE OF MINIMUMS

That which is most tender
can overcome that which is most rigid.
That which has least substance
can penetrate that which has least space.

Acting without deliberate action,
and teaching without uttering a word
are rarely practiced.
So few find their way to the Great Integrity!

COMMENTARY

Most of us become addicted to maximums —
maximum possessions, maximum power,
maximum praise, and maximum leisure.
Although they are toxic, they function as
compulsive compensations for our inability to
fulfill our human needs. Lao Tzu sings the praises
of minimums inviting us to appreciate their higher
value. Nevertheless, he never expresses blame or
guilt when we choose the maximums instead. He
only observes that most of us are by and large
making poor choices. He probably sensed that
higher alternative values cannot resonate widely
until we all grow up in families and communities
that nurture these values.

Which do you value more –
your wealth or your wellness?
Which is more harmful –
to lead or to lose?

The greater is your attachment,
the more bereft is your release.
The more you hoard,
the less is left to enjoy.

Those on the path
to the Great Integrity
flow without forcing,
leaving no space for disasters.

COMMENTARY

Most people, given the opportunity, would choose wealth over wellness, winning over losing. They cling desperately and dependently in their close relationships, and hoard their possessions. These are choices, says Lao Tzu, that lead to disaster. Our alternative is to flow without forcing, and to release ourselves from our false values and counter-productive behaviors. As in Verse 43, we are reminded of the choices and values that can help to direct us toward the path leading to the Great Integrity. However, to stay the course, people from everywhere need to join us.

Verse 45 ILLUSION AND REALITY

Completeness can seem incomplete,
yet the completeness that we achieve
can be remarkable.
Fullness can seem empty,
yet the fullness that we achieve
can be very useful.

Truth can appear as lie.
Straightness can appear as twisted.
Skillfulness can appear to be clumsy.
Eloquence can sound like foolishness.

But the dialectic of yin and yang
is not illusory.
Activity can overcome cold.
Tranquillity can overcome heat.
And peacefulness is the natural seed
of a violent world.

COMMENTARY

We live in a world of illusions, but not all is illusory. We live in a world of realities, but not all is real. That which is most illusory is our belief that everything must be either complete or incomplete, full or empty, straight or crooked, skillful or clumsy, eloquent or not. That which is most real is the experience of process, for example, of activity overcoming cold or of tranquillity overcoming heat.

In all processes, when one extreme is reached, its opposite is ripe to generate. The most significant potential process of our time is the re-establishment of the Great Integrity. Why? It is because extreme fragmentation, violence and cruelty have now become so prevalent.

Verse

46 ENOUGH IS ENOUGH!

When the Great Integrity
  permeated our lives,
freely galloping horses fertilized the fields.

When the Great Integrity was lost,
war horses were bred in the countryside.

There is no greater calamity
than acquisitiveness racing out of control.

Only those who know
  when enough is enough
can ever have enough.

COMMENTARY

There is no greater loss than that of the Great Integrity. Since we have exchanged it for the curse of greed, we have inherited all manner of social calamities. Our insatiable desires for possessions, and our compensatory psyches binging to feed our starving egos, have bred a perverted consciousness to navigate a perverted world. Rebirthing our world as a cooperating global village, and rebirthing our consciousness as the Great Integrity, can recreate our awareness of when enough is enough. Only then will we be released from the omnipresent prisons of selfishness in which we have all been trapped during this temporary five thousand-year era of civilizations as we have known them.

47 GOING BEYOND

We can understand the world as it is
without leaving our home.
We can understand the world as it might be
without peering dreamily out our window.

The further we go,
the less we know.

Wise people understand the 10,000 things
without going to each one.
They know them
   without having to look at each one,
and they transform all
   without acting on each one.

COMMENTARY

Since our main problem in life is transcending our inherited pathological institutions and their rationales, it is counterproductive to immerse ourselves in all their perverted details. We don't have to experience every toxic habit and premise. To transcend our present way of life requires our creating alternative ways of relating to each other and new holistic ways of thinking. Endlessly traveling all the old roads and peering through all the old windows will tend only to lock us more tightly into our past.

Another implication of this verse is the need to release ourselves from the naïve illusions of pragmatism. These illusions urge us to rely upon our direct experience as the basis for our premises, conclusions and actions. Lao Tzu has no trust in understandings that come solely out of our perceptions, or out of coercive actions that derive from our desires — however well-observed are the perceptions, and however well-intentioned are the actions.

Verse

48 ALL IS DONE WITHOUT DOING

To obtain a diploma
    requires the storage of trivia.
To obtain the Great Integrity
    requires its abandonment.

The more we are released
    from vested fragments of knowledge,
the less we are compelled
    to take vested actions,
until all is done without doing.

When the ego interferes
in the rhythms of process,
there is so much doing!
But nothing is done.

COMMENTARY

Is Lao Tzu stuck in a literary mannerism involving paradox? Or is there a deep insight into the concept of "all is done without doing", a repeated premise in many of these eighty-one verses?

What Lao Tzu means by "doing" is acting against the rhythms of natural processes and against the pretended natural inertia and laziness of human beings, to make something happen. That means that "doing" implies actions impelled by interference, force and coercion. Such actions are always in opposition to natural processes, and usually in violation of human needs and well-being.

What Lao Tzu means by "getting done" is to flow with and facilitate natural processes, and never violate the needs and harmony of human beings in the process of producing the needs of the community. "Getting done" is always cooperating with nature and with other people. "Doing" is always a violation of nature and the exploitation of other people.

Therefore what he means by "all is done without doing" is that everything is accomplished without coercion.

Furthermore, there is a coincidence between form and content when Lao Tzu expresses the idea in *paradox* rather than *logic*.

Logic is the province of the left cerebral hemisphere,[36] which functions through verbal commands. It is the medium for the scientific method, which requires that experimenters divorce themselves from the subject of their investigation so that they can manipulate and control the conditions of their experiment, and observe the outcomes as an outsider. *Paradox*, on the other hand, is the province of the more intuitive and holistic right cerebral hemisphere. It is the medium for artists who merge with their work in the process of creation. Artists who carefully plan all the details of their work in advance of the creative process are acting more like scientists, predominantly engaging their left logical brain, and thus preventing their work from emerging spontaneously "without doing".

What Lao Tzu is always concerned with is the re-establishment of the Great Integrity. For him, the Great Integrity is the return to intuition and the merging of self and non-self. For us, having evolved to a different stage of evolution, we don't want to throw away our hundreds of years of scientific experience. For us, our return to the Great Integrity means an integrity at a much higher level than Lao Tzu could imagine. Our Great Integrity is to integrate our now advanced scientific left brain with our intuitive artistic right brain. For us, returning to the Great Integrity is to end our schizoid patterns of acting and thinking by establishing a planetary community in which cooperation replaces competition, war between countries becomes an anachronism because there will be no separate countries, and where all the fragmentations and coercive acts of the past will be exchanged for a Great Integrity beyond the wildest dreams of Lao Tzu.

Verse 49 WISDOM

Wise people are not absorbed
   in their own needs.
They take the needs of all people
   as their own.

They are good to the good.
But they are also good
   to those who are still absorbed
   in their own needs.

Why?
Because goodness is in the very nature
   of the Great Integrity.

Wise people trust those who trust.
But they also trust those who do not trust.

Why?
Because trusting is in the very nature
   of the Great Integrity.

Wise people merge with all others
rather than stand apart judgmentally.
In this way, all begin
   to open their ears and hearts,
more prepared to return
   to the innocence of childhood.

COMMENTARY

One premise here is that wisdom and humanity require the ability to subordinate one's own ego demands, personal needs and predilections in order to identify with the needs of all people.

A second implied premise is that no matter how each of us may in some ways become corrupted by social demands, bribes and indoctrinations, there is an innate humanity somewhere in the core of every human being.

A third implied premise is that by addressing this human Essence in each person, we prevent ourselves from becoming cynics, and allow those of us who have become corrupted to return to our essential human nature, that is, to the innocence of our childhood.

Verse
50 THE FORCES OF LIFE AND DEATH

Every one of us is born,
and everyone dies.

However, three of every ten
seem to be born to live,
three seem to be born to die,
and three live lifefully or deathfully
according to their chosen life styles.

But only one in ten
seems to survive all dangers.
When walking through the jungle,
she never fears the rhinoceros
because there seems to be
*   no place in her to butt his horns.*
She never fears the tiger
because there seems to be
*   no place to sink his claws,*
and she never fears weapons
because there seems to be
*   no place their steel can penetrate.*

This is the fulfilled person
*   of the Great Integrity*
who leaves no space in life
*   for premature death.*

COMMENTARY

Chinese medicine identifies two main sources of Vital Energy (*Qi*) that determine our ability to survive adversity. The first is called *Yuan* or *Genetic Qi*. It is the Vital Energy we inherit from our parents. The second is called *Hou Tian Zhi* or *Acquired Qi*. It is the Vital Energy that derives from our life style, that is, from the air we breathe, the food and drink we ingest, our exposure to the sun and its full spectrum light, our actions and emotions through which we relate to others and to our environment, and the people and their Qi with whom we most directly intersect.

Four kinds of people are differentiated here according to their life force which protects them, or their death force which threatens them.

(1) Those who seem to have been "born to live". These are the three of every ten people who Lao Tzu identifies as having inherited a strong Yuan Qi from their parents.

(2) Those who seem to have been "born to die" because they seem not to have "selected" their parents so wisely.

(3) Those whose choice of life style determines whether they live "lifefully" or "deathfully". Those who lead a life style that supports their Vital Energy thereby facilitate their own health and longevity, while those who lead a life style that challenges and insults their Vital Energy weaken their health and invite an early death.

(4) Lastly, are those who seem to be impervious to harm and premature death because they live in harmony with others, with the universe and with themselves. This, of course is living in the Great Integrity. Today, although we might be fortunate in inheriting a strong genetic Qi, and we might choose our life styles relatively wisely, we cannot live entirely in the Great Integrity because our social environment is more or less a contradiction of the Great Integrity. This contradiction is manifested in most of our institutions, whether family, work, religion, schooling, sports, leisure, politics, economics, medical care, or whatever. Since we are all social beings and cannot avoid growing up in the womb of these predominantly corrupt institutions, the nearest we can come to living the Great Integrity is by rejecting many of their values, premises and behaviors. Instead, we can follow Lao Tzu's alternative consciousness, transforming our own personal lives as we participate in the transformation of our institutions. It is only after we succeed in attaining these goals that any of us will be "walking the waters", never fearing that weapons will harm us, because there will be no harmful weapons in a planet that embraces the Great Integrity.

51 NATURAL BIRTHING

All in the universe
    derive from the Primal Integrity.
The interaction of yin and yang
    shapes and nourishes them,
and evolution ever transforms them
in their endless ecological dance.

Therefore, in its own way,
every entity celebrates its Primal Mother.
Not out of any mandate.
Not out of any obligation.
But solely as the expression
    of its own integrity.

COMMENTARY

The way of the Tao – the great, undifferentiated universe and Mother of all entities – is natural, spontaneous and unconscious. Contrary to current human relationships, this Great Integrity is not acknowledged by mandate or obligation, but only as an "is-ness". This verse, thereby refers to the integrity of all life including us human beings before we left our metaphoric "Garden of Eden" that we shared with all other life on the planet. We were separated from the universal "Garden" by acquiring knowledge, that is, self-consciousness, differentiating ourselves from all that is *Not-Us*.

By excluding us civilized human beings in this verse, we are reminded how natural and universal is the Great Integrity when you remove us from the picture.

Only we modern homo sapiens traded the Great Integrity for its opposite: the Great Alienation, which has resulted in our victimizing nature, each other, and of course, ourselves. It is only we who have brought misery into the world as a product of selling our Integrity to the metaphoric devil who is the incarnation of every form of fragmentation.

The question that Lao Tzu never does raise, because each generation asks only the questions it is capable of solving, is: now that we humans have lost the Great Integrity and thereby created gross ugliness and suffering, and more recently, even the capability of destroying most life on this once thriving planet, what is to be done?

How can we neutralize our own satanic power? Lao Tzu has no strategic answer. But we do. It is to rewrite and live Lao Tzu's *Theory and Practice of the Great Integrity*. Unless we do, there might not be any recovery of the Great Integrity or any twenty-second century for us.

Verse 52 RETURNING TO OUR ORIGINS

Everything has a common origin
that we might call
the Mother of the Universe.

Once in pre-conscious times,
we were all a part of this Mother,
just as we – all her children –
    were part of each other.

This was when we were all
umbilically still attached
to the Great Integrity.

Some thousands of years ago,
    our species alone
issued a declaration of independence
    from our Mother.
Now it is time to reunite with her.

Thereafter, we will never any more suffer
the 10,000 miseries
that only we human beings have acquired.

Block all the loopholes!
Shut all the doors to the old temptations!
And we will never again feel deprived.

If we crawl through the loopholes,
if we race through the gate
    back to the 10,000 addictions,
we will never be fulfilled.

How shall we know the Great Integrity?
When our insights proliferate
    even in the smallest matters.
When our strength is boundless
    even while ever yielding.

We can keep our outsights
    when returning to our insights.
In this way, we will reharmonize
    with our Mother,
celebrating the Great Integrity
    on a higher level.

COMMENTARY

In the beginning was the wordless unity of every entity with Mother Nature.[37]

Billions of years and millions of species later came the innocent word generated in the social-body-minds of our hominid ancestors.

Several millions of years still later, with the advent of civilizations as we have known them, came the coercive word[38] which rationalized the inequities that history has called "progress".

This progress might now be defined as an incredibly advanced technology. It is a great paradox that it is this very technology, although we sacrificed our humanity for it, that might provide us with one of the main prerequisites for planetary abundance, peace, and community, and thereby the recovery of our lost humanity.

The last stanza proposes that if we keep our *outsights* (the knowledge we have accumulated from our scientific and technological discoveries) when we return to our *insights* (our reharmonization with each other, with nature and with ourselves), we will celebrate the Great Integrity on a higher level than any species in the entire evolution of life on this planet, even though our species was the only one that ever lost it.

53 NOT YET ON THE WAY

Those who have the smallest grain of wisdom
would want to walk the simple path
  of the Great Integrity.
Their only fear would be to go astray.

Indeed, there is a good reason to fear
when most of the world
  is piled into two wagons
racing toward each other on a single lane road.

In one over-crowded wagon
  is the vast majority
who live in weedy fields
with empty granaries.

In the other wagon are those
  whose garments are opulently embroidered.
They gorge themselves on rich foods
  far beyond their appetites,
and guzzle their inebriating drinks
  far beyond their thirst.

They accumulate wealth
even beyond their avaricious cravings
while armed to the teeth
  against their starving neighbors.

Surely such thievish degradation
couldn't be the way to the Great Integration.

COMMENTARY

What could be more in contradiction to the Great Integrity than our civilizations, which for the past few thousand years have been divided into the over-privileged, and the underprivileged, with these inequities maintained by armed police, courts and prisons called our system of "justice".

The last line which acknowledges the impossibility of such a depraved way of life ever leading to the Great Integrity is rhymed out of deference to the original which makes a pun of the word *tao* which is both the Chinese word for the *Great Integrity* as well as the word for *thievery*, with both meanings of *tao* utilizing the same intonation (the fourth tone).

Verse 54 THE WHOLE IS IN EACH PART

Whatever is planted deeply
    is not easily uprooted.
Whatever is embraced sincerely
    does not crave escape.
Ever since we lost our intuition
    as our main guide in life,
these virtues have had to be
    consciously cultivated to survive.

Cultivate them in yourself
    and they will be genuine.
Cultivate them in your family
    and they will surely flourish.
Cultivate them in your community
    and they will be long lasting.
Cultivate them in your country
    and they will be widely propagated.
Cultivate them in the world
    and they will certainly become universal.

In this way you will know others
    by what you do yourself.
You will know families
    by what you contribute as a family.
You will know the world
    by what you do as a planetary citizen.

How do we know all this?
Because we know that each part is the whole,
and the whole is in each part.

COMMENTARY

There are three main insights shared in the verse:

(1) That once we all practiced the Great Integrity. This was in prehistoric times when we were one with nature and each other.

(2) That now that we have lost our intuition as our main guide to decision-making, the only way we can re-establish our integrity is through the conscious cultivation of alternative behaviors.

(3) That if we are to acquire a truly holistic consciousness, it cannot be done only through self-enlightenment, or only by creating a more democratic political structure. We must transform and transcend at every level – as individuals, as families, as communities and as a planetary village. The further implication here is that there is no sequential formula that will work. That is, individual enlightenment will not, by itself, lead to planetary community, nor will institutional change, by itself, lead to our transformation from selfish to integral personalities. All levels of transformation must evolute in tandem *because we know that each part is the whole and the whole is in each part*.

Verse

55 THE PROMISES OF THE GREAT INTEGRITY

When we will live in complete integrity
we will be innocent like newborn babies.
Wasps and scorpions will not sting us.
Wild beasts will not maul us.
Birds of prey will not seize us.

Our bones will be pliable,
our sinews soft.
Yet our grip will be firm.
Even before we have known conjugality,
our sexuality will be easily aroused
    because we will be so virile.

We'll sing all day long
    without becoming hoarse
because we'll be in full harmony.
To be in harmony
is to live in the Great Integrity.
To live in the Great Integrity
    is the ultimate wisdom.

However, to interfere with nature
    is to seek control.
To seek control is to create dis-stress.
To create dis-stress produces exhaustion.
All these negations of the Great Integrity
also negate life and its longevity.

COMMENTARY

Living in the Great Integrity is living in harmony with nature, with each other and with ourselves. This harmony defines an integrity that will allow us to transcend both our self-imposed antagonisms with nature as well as the present limitations of our physical, sexual, artistic, intellectual and spiritual capacities.

However, when we seek to coerce nature, each other and ourselves, as is typical in our present life-styles, we create conditions of dis-stress, producing tendencies toward exhaustion, illness, and the negations of the very meaning, potentiality and longevity of our lives.

244

Verse
56 HOW TO PREPARE FOR THE GREAT INTEGRITY

Those who know don't lecture.
Those who lecture don't know.

To prepare the way for the Great Integrity –
Close the rationalizing routes!
Shut the gloomy gates!
Blunt the sharp edges!
Release those who are tethered!
Soften the blinding lights!
Unite the world!

We cannot achieve the Great Integrity
through intimacy or emotional detachment,
nor through posturing or humility.

Since the Great Integrity
   makes no judgments or demands,
how will we know when it has arrived?
When it permeates us
   with its universal "is-ness".

COMMENTARY

How do we prepare the way for the Great Integrity? Certainly not through lecturing, because "those who lecture don't know".

Then how?

By giving up rationalizing, by laughing, by eliminating our sharp antagonisms, by re-educating and releasing those who are imprisoned, by burying blame and revenge, and by giving up our coercive relations.

Lao Tzu reminds us that we cannot achieve the Great Integrity through either intimacy or detachment, nor through force or humility.

And how will we know when it has arrived? *When it permeates us with its universal "is-ness".*

57 SIMPLICITY BLOSSOMS
WHEN COERCION DIES

Govern a state with predictable actions.
Fight a war with surprise attacks.
But the universe becomes ours
only by eliminating coercive acts.
By not doing, nothing lacks.

How do we know these lessons?
By tuning into our Essence.

The more taboos and prohibitions there are,
the poorer the people become.
The more deadly weapons there are,
the more our fears turn us numb.

When craftiness spreads far,
the more bizarre what is done,
The stricter the laws there are,
the less the robbers run.

Therefore, the wise know
to make no one a foe.
The less coercing we do,
The more tranquillities grow.

When harmony reigns,
and we rule ourselves with felicity,
everyone gains,
and we'll all live in simplicity.

COMMENTARY

There is a popular saying that money is the root of all evil. That's a cover-up. The real root of all evil is coercion. Money is the bribe that enforces inequitable exchanges. When bribes are insufficient, then brute force becomes the *modus vivendi*.

If coercion is the enemy, then cooperation is the liberator. When coercion dies, the Great Integrity is reborn. *When harmony reigns, and we rule ourselves with felicity, everyone gains, and we'll all live in simplicity.*

Verse 58 ALTERNATIVES

When a government is more benign,
the people are more productive.
When a government is more tyrannical,
the people are more rebellious.

But whatever the government,
if disaster is the bitter fruit
    of others' good fortune,
how long can such injustice be tolerated?
How long we have endured the hypocrisies!

Those pretending to be righteous
    act deceitfully.
Those pretending to be religious
    revert to evil.
We have been deluded!
And each day it becomes worse!

Be firm and armed, but do no harm!
Be as sharp as a knife, but do not cut!
Be ready to transform, but do not provoke!
Illuminate the darkness of ignorance,
    but do not blind!

COMMENTARY

Even in Lao Tzu's time, the impoverishment of some people was the source of others' good fortune. These injustices, he says, were rationalized by deceits which have deluded the people for so long! It seems that each day from Lao Tzu's time to our own, the hypocrisies have continued to escalate. Since there are about one million days that have intervened, one could say that we have become separated from the Great Integrity about one million times further than those who lived in the sixth century BCE!

What shall we do? Lao Tzu's advice in the last stanza is still sound. We need to be firm, clear and prepared to transform our lives, but the process should be one without arrogance or provocation, never victimizing others as we have been victimized.

59 THE IMPORTANCE OF MODERATION

To serve humanity,
there is nothing more important
    than to be moderate.

To be moderate
is to return to the female yin principle.

To return to the yin
is to become nurturing.

To be nurturing
is to acquire enormous capacity.

To have enormous capacity
is to be ready for the Great Integrity.

To be ready for the Great Integrity
is to be ready to serve humanity.

In this way we will become firmly planted
    in the Great Integrity,
the pathway to a clear vision and a long life.

COMMENTARY

This verse is all about the synergy of our visions for the future and our present life styles. The Great Integrity is a universal nurturing of our common identity, that is, the predominance of the yin cooperating harmony of all entities. How do we ready ourselves for the Great Integrity? By practicing moderation and nurturing peace, cooperation, love and integrity in our hearts, dreams and everyday lives.

Verse
60 OUR FUTURE

Govern a country
  like you would fry a small fish –
with care, respect
  and with the least interference.

When the world is governed
  according to the Great Integrity,
evil will lose its power.

Not only will evil lose its power,
it will no longer even exist.

When evil ceases to exist,
neither will good exist.

Without good and evil,
we simply will live totally
  in our human natures.

No one will compromise anyone else
because we will all be
  inextricable parts of the Great Integrity.

COMMENTARY

Governing a large country with the tender care that is needed to fry a small fish is a preparation of our minds, hearts and behaviors to live in the Great Integrity.

When we finally do achieve the Great Integrity, there will be no separate countries, and certainly no politicians will be needed to govern over us. Then there will be no evil, that is, coercive behaviors and institutions that force people to live inequitably.

When *evil* no longer exists, its opposite, *good*, also ceases to have any meaning.[39] Therefore, when we finally re-establish the Great Integrity, we human beings will live without good and evil, just as every other species on our planet. Instead, we will simply be liberated to express our human natures in all our thoughts, feelings and activities.[40]

In our era when the Great Integrity
has been lost,
separate states have arisen.
Some become very large.
Others remain very small.

When the larger ones
try to conquer the small,
at first the smaller ones are defeated
even though yang aggression
meets yang resistance.
But death stalks the people
on both sides of war.

Is it not better for great countries to be
like vast low lying lands
into which all streams passively go?

And the smaller countries,
like the innocent streams,
can be welcomed at the end of their passage
by wide open arms,
calmly receiving their flow?

Would not this mutual humility
save countless lives now,
while serving as a rehearsal
for the coming of the Tao?

COMMENTARY

From the time of Lao Tzu to our own day, our planet has been carved up by superpowers that have subjugated smaller countries to serve their own selfish needs. Today, superpowers are anachronistic. Just as hominid hordes evolved into clans, and clans evolved into tribes, and tribes into city-states, and city-states into countries, our time is the evolutionary moment for countries to dissolve into a single planetary community expressing the Great Integrity.

In Lao Tzu's time such an evolutionary step was only a utopian wish that could not yet be realized. So here in this verse the great ancient wise man shares his dreams, providing idealistic alternatives that he must have known could not be realized in his time. Because we are the first generations that can put these dreams into practice, how much more intensively and realistically do Lao Tzu's words echo in our ears, minds and hearts than they did for Lao Tzu's own contemporaries?

It is obvious that globalization defines the evolutionary stage of our twenty-first century. The question that has not been resolved is whose globalization will it be? That which will serve transnational, international and superpower hegemonies? Or a global village where the Great Integrity will at last fulfill the hearts and dreams of all humanity and the needs of our universal Mother – the Great Ecology that defines and embraces all life on our planet?

62 REHEARSALS FOR THE GREAT INTEGRITY

The Great Integrity is the sanctuary
of all human beings.

For those who are honest and caring,
it is a guide and a treasure.

For those who are dishonest and deceitful,
it is also a treasure because a good word
    can rationalize a selfish act,
and because a good act, now and then,
can serve as a mask for living extravagantly
from the misery of others.

Since the Great Integrity
    is so universally acknowledged,
don't cast away those
    who use it opportunistically.
Rather cast away the opportunities
    to live selfishly so that the Great Integrity
    can more fully permeate all our lives.

We might begin with the inauguration
    ceremonies of our leaders.
Instead of showering them
    with precious gifts,
instead of the public swearing
    of meaningless oaths,
why not share a meditation
    on the Great Integrity as a prelude
    to its comprehensive embrace?

COMMENTARY

The main premise here is that no human being is born evil. As other verses explicitly state, it is quite the opposite. We are all born as innocent inextricable parts of the Great Integrity, incapable of any corrupt act. We learn to be dishonest from a society that rewards deceit. Lao Tzu suggests that therefore don't reject any person, but rather cast away the opportunities to live selfishly. Then the Great Integrity will more and more permeate our lives, fulfilling our essential natures and needs.

Of course, such a premise is opposite to the doctrine that we all inherit the original sin of Adam and Eve. Had Lao Tzu known of Genesis, he might have proposed that the expulsion of Adam and Eve from the Garden of Eden was a metaphor, not about eating from the tree of knowing and reason, but from consuming the fruit of rationalization to justify the institutionalization of inequities among human beings. Lao Tzu argues that our solution to corruption and immorality is not to cast away human beings, but to cast away the system of temptations and opportunities to abuse others.

But the fundamentalists among us would say that Genesis is no metaphor. It is a literal historical account. Since belief cannot be a productive subject for debate, we might shift the discussion to a question of good humored and non-judgmental facetious levity: how in all these centuries of religious paintings has Eve always inherited a navel?

Verse

63 THE SECRETS OF GETTING THINGS DONE

Act without acting on.
Work without working at.

Enter bountifulness
*   when it is still insufficiency.*
Answer with kindness
*   when faced with hostility.*

Begin a difficult task in its easy stage
because large problems grow from small ones.

Begin a large task in its formative state
because complex issues
*   originate from simple ones.*

But beware of those who promise
*   quick and easy solutions!*
Accept problems as challenges.

In this way, the sage accomplishes great tasks
without ever having to struggle with them.

COMMENTARY

Lao Tzu's secrets for getting things done are: 1) act without acting on, 2) work without working at, 3) begin at the early stages of a process, 4) answer hostility with kindness, and 5) avoid illusory easy solutions.

What he means by *acting without acting on, working without working at,* and *accomplishing without ever having to struggle* is to become part of processes in motion rather than to work against processes. *Acting on, working at,* and *struggling with* are all coercive activities, and Lao Tzu's most important advice in life is to avoid coercion. It is, of course, precisely opposite to how most of our institutions are programmed. Young people, for the most part, go to school because they are required to do so. Adults go to work because, if they don't, they will not receive the necessities of life. Most people go to church because they believe that if they don't go, they won't get into heaven. Most people don't commit crimes, because, if they do, they will go to prison. Even most babies and young children are accommodated to the system of coercion by physical punishment when they do something that displeases their parents. Lao Tzu says all this is wrong. The use of force indoctrinates us into behaving contrary to our human natures and contrary to the Great Integrity.

Line 3 in the extant Chinese version is omitted because it seems irrelevant to the rest of the verse and incomprehensible. It reads: "Taste without tasting".

Verse 64 TIMING

It is easy to hold what is still stable.
It is easy to mold what is not yet formed.
It is easy to shatter what is still fragile.
It is easy to scatter what is yet light and small.
Therefore, act now rather than wait.
Get things done before it's too late.

A huge tree that you can't get your arms around
grows from a tiny seedling birth.
A tower of nine stories high
rises from a small heap of earth.

A thousand mile journey begins with one step.
This is an ancient tale.
Those who procrastinate,
And those who take premature actions fail.

Those who interfere in processes disrupt them.
Those who hold tightly to possessions
     lose everything.
Wise people succeed
     because they never force an outcome.
They never suffer a loss
     because they are not attached to anything.

Many succeed in gathering a few assets.
But when the stakes begin to sail,
     and greed crashes
Through all cautionary boundaries,
     failures unmercifully prevail.

Wise people don't accumulate possessions,
or teach anyone to amass things.
They devote themselves to the natural rhythms
that the Great Integrity brings.

COMMENTARY

Timing for Lao Tzu is always a matter of becoming in tune with the natural rhythms of processes. To do so is to avoid all premature or procrastinated actions, as well as to avoid corrupting and disrupting these processes. As we would say in our modern colloquial vernacular — *Go with the flow!*

In ancient times,
before there were those who were governed,
and those who governed over,
the sage blended with others,
and all was done
    through the Primal Simplicity.
People lived in innocence.

When the Great Fragmentation
replaced the Great Integrity,
cleverness defeated wisdom.
Even some enlightened sages
became victims of the rulers
commanding the highest intrigue.

COMMENTARY

Two eras are contrasted: 1) *ancient times*,[41] before there were castes and classes dividing human beings, and when tribal people *lived in innocence*, and 2) civilized times *when the Great Fragmentation replaced the Great Integrity*, and when the rulers and intellectuals traded wisdom for cleverness. In this second era, the over-privileged has utilized the *highest intrigue* to gain and sustain power over everyone else — even over some formerly enlightened sages.

Verse 66 WISDOM ALWAYS COMES FROM BELOW

Why do all the hundreds of great rivers
flow naturally to the sea?
Because the sea is always lower
    than the rivers.

When are thousands of people
    attracted to a sage?
When she positions herself below them,
always listening, tirelessly responding
    to their needs.

Never commanding.
Never coercing.
Never manipulating.

Such a sage is forever adored.
Since she treats everyone
    with love and respect,
everyone loves and respects her.

COMMENTARY

This is a simple ode to mutual love, respect, humility, devotion, responsiveness, and to always being there to listen to and care for each other. Such wisdom of behavior is such an antithesis to our all too common social relations, which are often characterized by *commanding, coercing and manipulating* each other.

Verse 67 THE THREE TREASURES

When most people hear
        about the Great Integrity,
they say it is useless folly.
Because it is not like anything
        in the world we know,
they also find it inconceivable.

On the contrary!
The Great Integrity has given us
three treasures to cherish:
The first is love.
The second is moderation.
The third is humility.

If you love,
you will be fearless.
If you are moderate,
you might always sense abundance in life.
If you live in humility,
you will be widely trusted.

But you will not have the capacity to love
if you are fearful.
Even worse, if you are fearless
        and without love,
you will always be courting disaster.

If you live in insufficiency,
you have no opportunity to be moderate.
If you live in overabundance,
you not only live immoderately,
but are always courting disaster.

If no one trusts you,
then compensatory ego will preclude humility.
If everyone trusts you,
and you lack humility,
you will always court disaster.

The three treasures
        are practical guides to the Great Integrity.
The greatest foolishness
        is to live without them.

COMMENTARY

The three treasures are both expressions of the Great Integrity as well as prerequisites for achieving it. They are also interrelated and inextricable from each other. In fact, it is not possible to fully achieve one without also achieving the other two.

Love is the primary treasure. It is the very heart of the Great Integrity. It is our ability to fully identify and empathize with the wondrous beings and entities of this remarkable universe. But love requires a combination of fearlessness and assertiveness along with caring and empathy. If we are fearful, our timidity blocks our freedom to express the love in our hearts. If we are fearless, but lack caring and empathy, then we always court disaster to ourselves and to all with whom we relate.

Moderation, like love, is a natural treasure of the Great Integrity. It is when competition and extreme mal-distributions of wealth replace cooperation and equitable divisions of the community's resources that moderation is sacrificed to greed and insufficiency. Those who live in insufficiency never have the opportunity to be moderate, and those who live in overabundance allow their greed to rob them of this treasure, thereby also courting disaster for themselves and others.

Humility is the third treasure. If our lives are governed by our egos, there is no space for humility. The excessive expression of our egos is a compensation for the starvation of our humanity and for our need to be appreciated, and also as a means to coerce others. Lao Tzu says if no one trusts us because of our inflated egos, we sacrifice ever being able to acquire this third treasure. However, if people do trust us, even if we fail to relate to others in humility, then we will bring on a third way of courting disaster.

Lao Tzu characterizes these three treasures as *practical guides to the Great Integrity*. He reminds us that living without them is the greatest foolishness because we thereby deny ourselves the very humanity that is essential to fulfill our lives.

THE ETHICS OF WAR

The best soldier fights
without vengeance,
without anger
and without hate.

He puts himself humbly
below his comrades,
thereby eliciting
the highest loyalty from them.

This is the power
of non-belligerence
and cooperation.
It is the ancient path to the Great Integrity.

COMMENTARY

As in so many verses, Lao Tzu focuses here on paradox. Soldiers are known for their vengefulness, anger, hate, arrogance and belligerence. His ideal soldier transcends these qualities because, in spite of his profession, he is on the ancient path to the Great Integrity.

Lao Tzu assumes that in "this period"[42] when the Great Integrity is violated by all nations and civilizations, war is an on-going part of the "normal" misery of life. However, he differentiates between just and unjust acts of war. War is justified only to defend against acts of aggression, and even then only if committed without anger or hate.

There is a story that Ram Das tells about a famous Japanese samurai who was murdered by a violent criminal. The samurai's disciple vowed to rid the world of this evil man so that he could never murder anyone else. It took him years of searching before finally he found this criminal. The samurai drew his sword, and as he was about to fulfill his vow, the criminal spit in his face, which, of course, made him very angry. He placed his sword back in its scabbard and calmly left the room rather than kill someone in anger.

Verse 69 IN WAR THE DEFENDER WILL BE VICTORIOUS

There is a saying among those wise in
    military affairs:
"We do not act as host taking the initiative,
but would rather be the guest
    assuming the defensive posture.
Rather than advancing one inch,
    we would rather retreat one foot."

This is called advancing without moving,
rolling up one's sleeves
    without baring one's arms,
fighting without weapons,
capturing the enemy without attacking.

There is no greater disaster
    than boasting of one's invincibility.
Such boasts lead to the loss
    of the Three Treasures.
Therefore, when two opposing sides
    meet in battle,
the one without an enemy will be victorious.

COMMENTARY

Lao Tzu reasserts his position that the only justification for war is defense, and that those who defend themselves against aggression will ultimately be victorious. Those who are the arrogant aggressors will not only ultimately lose the war, but will also lose the Three Treasures[43] of the Great Integrity.

Verse 70

SO EASY TO UNDERSTAND AND PRACTICE!

The Great Integrity is so easy to understand,
and so easy to practice.
Yet it is not understood.
Nor is it practiced.

It is not understood
because people's heads are filled
with 10,000 trivia and rationalizations,
leaving no space for anything else.

It is not practiced
because people are kept busy, though bored,
with the 10,000 corruptions and miseries
that leave no time for the Three Treasures.[44]

The Great Integrity is so ancient,
as old as the universe itself!
How can we expect people to remember it
after so many millennia of repression?

That is why
sages dress in rags
while they wear the Three Treasures
deep inside their hearts.

COMMENTARY

Lao Tzu points out here that although the Great Integrity is easy to understand and to practice, it is neither understood nor practiced.

It is not understood because for so many millennia our heads have been filled with artificial trivia and rationalizations, with no room for knowing the natural world.

It is not practiced because most of us are so caught up in all kinds of unproductive, superficial, and unfulfilling activities. Many are busily carrying out corrupt or misery producing actions or are the victims of such actions.

Lao Tzu also reminds us that a further difficulty in understanding and practicing the Great Integrity is that it has been repressed for thousands of years. *How can we expect people to remember it after so many millennia of repression?*

71 HEALING THE MIND

Academia confuses knowledge with knowing.
Most everyone applauds the memorization
*   of the 10,000 trivia.*
Beware! These schooled addictions
*   are not just myths –*
They are a form of mental illness.

Any fragment of the mind,
divorced from heart, spirit, human community,
and from the primal reality of the universe,
is an abomination of the Great Integrity.

Let us prepare for the Great Integrity
by cleansing ourselves of all these cobwebs
of cluttered fragments
*   that paralyze the mind.*
In this way we will function
*   as our own holistic physicians.*

COMMENTARY

Although the main intent of this verse is kept intact, some liberties have been taken in the translation to clarify why Lao Tzu identifies the memorization of "facts", not only as violations of the Great Integrity, but as a form of mental illness. We need to be our own holistic physicians to heal our fragmentized minds so they can join our hearts, spirits, human communities and primal reality in the Great Integrity.

72 COMPARING COERCIVE POWER AND THE EMPOWERMENT OF THE GREAT INTEGRITY

When people no longer fear
*   the power of governments,*
a far greater empowerment appears –
the Great Integrity –
which never needs to enforce itself.

Then, we will never again be driven
*   from our homes*
or be compelled to labor
*   for the benefit of others.*
We will all work naturally to fulfill ourselves,
and to meet our community needs.

In the Great Integrity,
we will all love ourselves and all others,
not as compensations
*   for ego deprivations and defilements,*
but as natural expressions of our humanity.

COMMENTARY

Here, as in Verse 71, the translation follows the general intent of the verse while expressing it in more modern terms. Lao Tzu compares life as experienced through coercive power with life when all people are fully empowered by the Great Integrity, that is, the freedom to fully love and serve oneself and all others as natural expressions of our human natures.

Again and again Lao Tzu returns to the basic proposition that our coercive way of life is an unnatural violation of the Great Integrity and of our essential humanity.[45] However, some day we'll live without coercion, celebrating each other *as natural expressions of our humanity.* The entire *Tao Te Ching* is an affirmation and commitment to this premise.

Verse
73 COURAGE, PATIENCE AND PARADOXES

The world we live in
  requires great courage and patience.
Those with great courage, but little patience,
  tend to kill or be killed.
Those with great courage
  as well as great patience
  will tend to survive.
But the Great Integrity never judges you
  for whatever path you happen to take.

The Great Integrity never strives
  but always fulfills itself,
never is commanded but always responds,
never is summoned but always appears,
never is impatient but all is done on time.

COMMENTARY

In this verse, Lao Tzu looks at life from two points of view.

In the first stanza he observes that because there is so much misery and conflict in the world, we must acquire great courage and patience to survive. When we acquire both courage and patience, we might survive, but, until we acquire the Great Integrity, the world will continue to generate misery and conflict. When we acquire great courage but lack patience, we endanger others and ourselves. He further observes that whichever of these survival mechanisms we use, the Great Integrity does not pass judgment upon us because each of us utilizes whatever defenses we have against the social condition we have inherited, and because blame and guilt are alien, and indeed toxic, to the Great Integrity.

In the second stanza, Lao Tzu observes the paradoxes of the world after we transform it. Then, living in the Great Integrity, we will fulfill ourselves naturally. We will respond without being commanded. We will appear without being coerced to be in any given place, and we will accomplish everything we need to do without being driven by that impatience which now originates in our being out of harmony with the very processes of which we are a part.

74 RULING BY FEAR

People do not fear death
when they are forced to live
    in hopeless misery,
Thereby the executioners are no threat
to fearless rebels who dare to make trouble.
They might even execute the executioners.

When people do fear death,
they do not defy the executioners at first.
But how long can the killings go on
before those who fear death
also become fearless?
Then, they too might execute
    the executioners.

By that time, the only ones left
who might serve as the executioners
would be the people themselves.
However, it is said that those who hew wood
in place of skilled carpenters
are likely to cut their own hands.

COMMENTARY

The ultimate problem for those who rule by fear and force is created when their rule produces such misery and hopelessness that their victims no longer fear death because life itself becomes worse then death. Then, the people rise up and rid the world of the professionals who are paid to keep them in misery. When there are no longer professionals to keep the people victimized, then the rulers are forced to bribe some of the people themselves to do the dirty work. But Lao Tzu reminds us that this won't work so well because, not being professionals, they will be more likely to hurt themselves than their own family and friends.

75 WHO CAN ENJOY THE TREASURES OF LIFE?

Why are the people so hungry?
Because their grain is devoured
by the rich in taxes.
That is why the people are starving.

Why are the people so rebellious?
Because the government deprives them
of their liberties and rights.
That's why the people are rebellious.

Why do the people not fear death?
Because their lives
are made so miserable
that death seems no worse than life.

Thus, no one can enjoy the treasures of life –
neither the rich
*   who squander their humanity,*
nor the government,
*   which tyrannizes the people,*
nor the people
*   who have nothing to gain from life.*

COMMENTARY

The translation here follows the original very closely until the last stanza which I believe successive translators may have altered to mystify the entire point of the verse out of fear of the consequences of openly criticizing the power elite.

For example, Gregory C. Richter provides a character-by-character translation of the last stanza as: "For those who do not use their life to act are able to value life."[46]

Jonathan Star's version is: "In the end, The treasure of life is missed by those who hold on and gained by those who let go."[47]

Clearly what this verse asks and answers is why people are starving, rebellious, and do not fear death. My departure from the last line of the extant Chinese text is to avoid its irrelevance to the rest of the Verse.

76 LET YIN PREDOMINATE OVER YANG [48]

When we are born,
we are soft and supple.
But when we've perished
there's no more tenderness
to be cherished.

When plants are young,
they are pliant and fragile.
When they die,
as they lose their green,
they wither and dry.

The sharp sword and knife
tryst always with death,
while love without strife
is an ever devoted
disciple of life.

An inflexible army
seals its own fate.
When a tree branch grows brittle,
it easily snaps,
whether long or little.

Wherever you go,
the rigid lie low.
While the weightless in the sky,
and all that is gentle,
fly boundlessly high.

COMMENTARY

This verse, like verses 5, 42, 45 and 78, elucidates the Chinese law of opposites: yin and yang, soft and hard, accepting and blaming, peace and war, harmony and antagonism.

The verse is a gentle metaphoric knock on the door of our consciousness, implying that hardness, inflexibility, war and coercion are not the nature of reality, but just the nature of our current social reality. Instead, we can make our lives peaceful, gentle, loving and flexible.

This verse also suggests that every extreme eventually turns into its opposite. Yin turns into yang and yang into yin. The entire evolution of species may be seen as five enormous evolutionary transformations: (1) From our *yang* origins of life in the sea as singled-cell amoeba-like creatures, to (2) the arising of *yin* plants always rooted somewhere, to (3) the transformation to complex *yang* sea fishes and then land animals, to (4) the development of more *yin* human beings living in communal clans and then tribes and more or less in harmony with nature, and (5) the birth of *yang* human beings in fiercely competitive groups, cities, states, countries, religions, ethnocentricities, egocentricities, and all manners of hostilities and animosities.

If we are going to survive the extreme forms of violence that we have now coupled with extremely high developments of technology, we need to enter our next, and probably for us human beings, our final evolutionary transformation as a planetary totally cooperative species who once more harmonizes with nature, with each other and within ourselves. However our transformation to the *yin* Great Integrity will be on a conscious, and therefore much higher level than any form of life has ever experienced before.

The prophetic wisdom of Lao Tzu relentlessly focuses on the shift in dominance from yang to yin – aggressive to yielding, from hard to soft, from war to peace, from hating to loving, and from hostile aggressive nations to a Great Universal Integrity. How unbelievable that it has taken us all these twenty-seven centuries to make this theory (*Tao*) and practice (*Te*) our guide book (*Ching*) to the first evolutionary leap that has ever been possible to effectuate consciously. Thank you, Lao Tzu, for creating our *Guide to the Theory and Practice of the Great Integrity*! If we follow it, all future generations will honor you and us. However, if we fail to create an alternative humane consciousness, and the appropriate social, economic and cultural institutions to nurture our new incredible technologies, there might not be any generations of the future to honor either you or us.

Verse
77 TWO OPPOSITE PROCESSES

The Way of the Great Integrity
is like stringing a bow,
pulling down the high,
lifting up the low –

Shortening the long,
lengthening the short
to take from the excessive
and give insufficiency support.

How opposite to our social norms
which increasingly impoverish the poor
to further enrich the rich
who do not need any more.

How can we gather the world's wealth
to create abundance for all in need?
Through rediscovering the Great Integrity,
by acting without praising the deed.

COMMENTARY

The Great Integrity always balances yin and yang, diminishing the surplus (yang) to normalize the deficiency (yin).

The process of the marketplace is opposite – selfish beyond bounds – always forcing the poor to create more wealth for the wealthy.

As the last stanza implies, rediscovering the Great Integrity is the key to the transcendence of all the inhumanities of our ever-widening inequities.

Verse 78 APPEARANCE AND REALITY

Nothing in the world
is softer and weaker than water.
Yet there is nothing better
for subduing all that is harder and stronger.

Everyone observes
  how weak overcomes strong,
how gentleness overcomes rigidity.
Yet, this principle is seldom
  put into conscious practice.

Though some may say it is useless,
to accept responsibility
for the calamities and toxicities of the world,
taking such responsibility
might put us on the road
  to the Great Integrity.
Just remember that truth
  often masquerades as falsity,
And falsity as truth.

COMMENTARY

There are three paradoxes that are juxtaposed here: 1) The paradox that water, which appears to be softer and weaker than anything else in the world, can subdue the hardest and strongest materials, like the huge rocks that the mountain stream disintegrates in its incessant flow. 2) The well-known paradox that *gentleness overcomes rigidity, yet this principle is seldom put into conscious practice*. Most of us resort to using verbal or physical force when confronted with resistance to our desires and needs. 3) The paradox that even though the calamities and toxicities we are subjected to in our daily lives come largely from the social condition we inherit, and that this condition might appear to be nothing we can do anything about, such an assumption may be false. We are reminded to *just remember that truth often masquerades as falsity, and falsity as truth.*

79 THE TOXICITY OF BLAME

Harboring a resentment
is sure to leave some resentment behind.
How can this be good?
It cannot.
Therefore, the wise accept all responsibility.

Although those who hold the power
keep blaming and bleeding the people,
the violated Great Integrity blames no one.
Once achieving the Great Integrity,
we will all function with a pure heart.

COMMENTARY

This verse is a continuation of the previous one, which also proposes that taking responsibility is an alternative to blame. Here the emphasis is on the toxic effects of harboring resentments. The verse also differentiates the present situation (applicable both for Lao Tzu's time and our own), in which injustice prevails, from the future when we will again experience the Great Integrity.

He also reminds us that as long as our social condition remains toxic, blaming those who blame and who take advantage of others, only adds to the toxicity. He dreams aloud of the future when, once achieving the Great Integrity, everyone will function with a pure heart, and no one will engage in blameful and shameful acts.

80 TRANSFORMING OUR LIVES

*Let us fashion small states
    with few inhabitants
who, without stress, can produce
    more than they require,
who are so happy with their lives
that they have no thought
    of migrating elsewhere –*

*Who inherit weapons and armor,
but have no need to use them,
who return to honest forms
    of communication,
and the simple enjoyments
    of an ecological way of life.*

*Although these states may be
    so close to each other
that they hear the barking
    of each other's dogs
and the crowing
    of each other's cocks,
living contentedly,
    they will have no need
    to invade each other's space.*

COMMENTARY

Coming toward the end of his argument for the Great Integrity, Lao Tzu simply states his utopian dream for a transition world of small non-competing states which produce all their needs without stress, and whose inhabitants live so contentedly, they have no need or desire to migrate to or invade their neighbors.

Today, this dream can come to fruition, not by going back to small states, but by creating a planetary village using an ultimate production and communication technology that is guided by a highly evolved consciousness and spirituality, all of which were beyond the wildest dreams of Lao Tzu.

Profound words are not clever.
Clever words are not profound.

Wise people are not quarrelsome.
Quarrelsome people are not wise.

Those who are intelligent are not ideologues.
Those who are ideologues are not intelligent.

The enlightened never hoard anything.
They share their possessions.

The more they give,
the greater their abundance.

The Great Integrity is the physician
     of the universe
who heals without harming
     and who acts without contention.

COMMENTARY

This last verse summarizes some of the paradoxes and corruptions of our present day life, reminding us of the incompatibilities of profundity and cleverness, wisdom and quarrelsomeness, intelligence and ideology, enlightenment and hoarding. In the last stanza, Lao Tzu casts a final hopeful glance at a possible future when we will live in the Great Integrity, and in which the physician of the universe will heal all the corruptions, allowing us to act naturally and in harmony with our environment, with each other and with ourselves. Of course, this physician is no one else but ourselves.

For us today, this final verse is a primal summary of the *Tao Te Ching* as our wake-up call, reminding us that we can no longer survive by cleverness, war, ideological rationalizations, and with our gross inequities. Twenty-seven centuries after Lao Tzu, we have at last created the technological basis for the Great Integrity: a potential planetary economy and communications capability of producing and distributing whatever human beings need anywhere on earth. We have only to transform our completely anachronistic social relations and consciousness, and release our long repressed spirituality.

Instead, we live in the greatest and most idiotic paradox of all time: we are utilizing the very technologies that can liberate us to create the most monstrous weapons of mass destruction that now threaten to murder every one of us on the planet.

In the entire evolution of species, every one except ours has been programmed by its genetics to live in accordance with its own nature. It is only we human beings who have evolved as a promise. Since we live largely according to our social development rather than our genetic commands, we fulfill our species potentials only to the extent that our social development actualizes these latencies. During our time on this planet, and especially in the last few hundred years, we have not only failed to realize our potentials, but we have been discovering more and more extreme methods of contradicting our human nature.

Lao Tzu's message to us is that we do not have to continue to live in contradiction to nature and to our human nature. We can live in accordance with the Great Integrity. For him, it was a remarkable insight and a utopian dream. For us, we have a choice — and not much time to make our decision — either we find our loving hearts, dreams and alternatives in Lao Tzu's Great Integrity or we will be the first species to become extinct through our own self-induced absurdity.

Selected English Editions

Blakney, R.B., *The Way of Life: Tao Te Ching by Lao Tzu*. Penguin, New York, 1955/83.

Bynner, Witter, *The Way of Life According to Lao Tzu: An American Version*. Capricorn Books, New York, 1944.

Carus, Paul, *The Teachings of Lao-Tzu: The Tao Te Ching*. St. Martin's Press, New York, 1913/2000.

Chan, Alan K.L., *Two Visions of the Way: A Study of the Wang Pi and Ho-shang Kung Commentaries on the Lao Tzu*. State University of New York Press, Albany, NY, 1991.

Chen, Ellen M., *The Tao Te Ching: A New Translation with Commentary*. Paragon House, New York, 1989.

Cheng, Man-jan, *Lectures on the Tao Teh Ching: My Words Are Very Easy To Understand* (trans. T.C. Gibbs) (Translation & Commentary). North Atlantic Books, Richmond, CA 1981.

Dalton, Jerry O., *Backward Down the Path: A New Approach to The Tao Te Ching*. Humanics Publishing Group, Atlanta, Georgia, 1994/1998.

Degen, Richard, *Tao Te Ching for the West*. Hohm Press, Prescott, Arizona, 1999.

Feng Gia-Fu, and English, Jane, *Lao Tsu — Tao Te Ching*. Random House, New York, 1972, Vintage Books, 1997.

Freke, Timothy, *Lao Tzu's Tao Te Ching*. Piatkus Books, 1995/1999.

Grigg, Ray, *The New Lao Tzu: A Contemporary Tao Te Ching*. Charles E. Tuttle, Boston, 1995.

Henricks, Robert G., *Lao-Tzu Te-Tao Ching: A New Translation Based on the Recently Discovered Ma-Wang-Tui Texts*. Ballantine Books, New York, 1992/1999.

Hinton, David, *Tao Te Ching: Lao Tzu*. Counterpoint Press, Washington, DC, 2000

Hwang, Shi Fu, *Tao Teh Ching: The Taoist's New Library*. Taoism Publishers, Austin, Texas, 1987/1991.

LaFargue, Michael, *The Tao of the Tao Te Ching: A Translation and Commentary*. State University of New York Publishers, Albany, New York, 1992.

Lau, D.C., *Lao Tzu — Tao Te Ching*. Penguin, London, 1964.

Mair, Victor H., *Tao Te Ching: The Classic Book of Integrity and the Way Based on the Recently Discovered Ma-Wang-Tui Manuscripts*. Bantam Books, London, 1990.

Miles, Thomas H., *Tao Te Ching — Lao Tzu: About the Way of Nature and its Powers*. Avery, Garden City Park, NY, 1992.

Mitchell, Stephen, *Tao Te Ching*. Harper & Row, New York, London, 1988/1992.

Ni, Hua-Ching, *Esoteric Tao Teh Ching*. College of Tao & Traditional Chinese Healing, Santa Monica, CA, 1992 and Sevenstar Communications Group, Santa Monica, CA, 1992.

Ni, Hua-Ching, *The Complete Works of Lao Tzu: Tao Teh Ching & Hua Hu Ching*. Sevenstar Communications Group, Santa Monica, CA, 1979/93

Pine, Red, *Lao-Tzu's Taoteching: With Selected Commentaries of the Past 2000 Years*. Mercury House, San Francisco, 1996/2001.

Ren Jiyu, *A Taoist Classic: The Book of Lao Zi*. Foreign Languages Press, Beijing, 1991/1995.

Star, Jonathan, *Tao Te Ching: The Definitive Edition (Translation & Commentary)*. Jeremy P. Tarcher/Putnam, New York, 2001.

Walker, Brian Browne, *The Tao Te Ching of Lao Tzu*. St. Martin's Press, New York, 1996.

Wilhelm, Richard, *Lao Tzu − Tao Te Ching: The Book of Meaning and Life*. Penguin, London, 1999.

Wu, John C., *Tao Teh Ching*. Shambhala Publications, London, 1989/1990.

Yutang, Lin, *The Wisdom of Laotse. (Translation & Commentary)* The Modern Library, New York, 1948/76.

VERBATIM TRANSLATIONS CONSULTED

Cheng, Yan: Manuscript 1996.

Johnson, Mark: Manuscript 1997.

Richter, Gregory C: *Gate of All Marvelous Things: A Guide to Reading the Tao Te Ching*. Red Mansions Publishing, South San Francisco, CA, 1998.

Star, Johathan: *Tao Te Ching: The Definitive Edition*. Jeremy P. Tarcher/Putnam, New York, 2001.

References

Auricular Acupuncture Therapy. Compiled by the Zoological Research Institute of the Chinese Academy of Science, 1972/74. (In Chinese).

Bahr FR: *The Chinese Meridians in their Projections on the Auricle* (wall chart). FR Bahr, Munich, Germany, 1999.

Bateson G: *Mind and Nature, A Necessary Unity.* Bantam, New York, 1979.

Bohm D: *Wholeness and the Implicate Order.* Routledge and Kegan Paul, London, 1980.

Bohm D, Weber R: "The Enfolding-Unfolding Universe: A Conversation with David Bohm". In K Wilber (ed) *The Holographic Paradigm and Other Paradoxes: Exploring the Leading Edge of Science.* Shambhala, Boston, 1985

Buck RM: *Cosmic Consciousness: A Classic Investigation of the Development of Man's Mystic Relationship to the Infinite.* EP Dutton, New York. 1969.

Caldicott H: *If you Love This Planet: A Plan to Heal the Earth.* WW Norton, New York and London, 1992.

Capra F: *The Tao of Physics.* Shambhala, Boston, 1975/85.
   : *The Turning Point.* Bantam, New York, 1982/88.

Chaisson, E: *The Life Era: Cosmic Selection and Conscious Evolution.* WW Norton, New York, 1989.

de Chardin T: *The Future of Man.* HarperCollins, New York 1959.

Csikszentmihalyi M: *The Evolving Self: A Psychology for the Third Millennium.* HarperCollins, New York, 1993.

Dale RA: "The Future of Music: An Investigation into the Evolution of Forms". *The Journal of Aesthetics and Art Criticism,* XXVI/4, 1968 (1)
   : "The Rise and Fall of the Scale: Toward a Social History of the Musical Scale". *Acta, International Congress of Aesthetics,* Stockholm, 1968 (2)
   : "The Micro-Meridians of the Ear and the Foot Acupuncture Systems". (with MD Huang) *American Journal of Chinese Medicine,* Vol 2, Suppl. 1. Proceedings of the Third World Symposium on Acupuncture and Chinese Medicine, 1975.
   : "The Micro-Acupuncture Systems: Part I." *American Journal of Acupuncture,* 1976; 4 (1): 7-24.
   : "The Micro-Acupuncture Systems Part II". *American Journal of Acupuncture,* 1976; 4(3): 207-227.
   : "The Origins and Future of Acupuncture". *American Journal of Acupuncture,* 1982; 10 (2): 101-120.
   "The Principles and Systems of Micro-Acupuncture". *International Journal of Chinese Medicine,* 1984; 1(4): 15-42.
   : "The Micro-Acupuncture Meridians". *International Journal of Chinese Medicine,* 1985; 2(2): 31-49.
   : *Dictionary of Acupuncture: Terms, Concepts and Points.* Dialectic Publishing, N. Miami Beach, FL, 1993.
   : "An Outline Evolution of Consciousness, Medicine and Social Relations". *Alternative*

Medicine Journal, 1995; 2 (5): 18-26.
: "The Systems, Holograms and Theory of Micro-Acupuncture". *American Journal of Acupuncture,* 1999; 27(3/4): 207-242.

Diamond J: *Guns, Germs, and Steel: The Fates of Human Societies.* WW Norton, New York, London, 1997/99.

Dossey L: *Space, Time & Medicine.* Shambhala, Boulder & London, 1982.

Drexler E and Peterson C with Pergamit G: *Unbounding the Future: The Nanotechnology Revolution.* William Morrow, New York, 1991.

Eisler R: *The Chalice and the Blade.* Harper, San Francisco, 1987.

Elgin D: *Awakening Earth: Exploring the Human Dimensions of Evolution.* William Morrow, New York, 1993.

Ferguson M: *The Aquarian Conspiracy: Personal and Social Transformation in Our Time.* Jeremy Tarcher/Putnam, New York, 1980/ 1987.

Frankl: V: *Man's Search for Meaning.* Washington Square Press, New York, 1985.

Fuller B: *Operating Manual for Space Ship Earth.* The Penguin Group, New York, 1991.

Gazzaniga, MS: "The Split Brain". *Man and The Nature of Consciousness,* ed RE Ornstein, Viking Press, 1973, pp 87-100.

Gollobin I: *Dialectical Materialism: Its Laws, Categories and Practice.* Petras Press, New York 1986.

Greene B: *The Elegant Universe: Superstrings, Hidden Dimensions, and the Quest for the Ultimate Theory.* WW Norton, New York & London, 1999.

Grof S: *The Adventure of Self-Discovery: Dimensions of Consciousness and New Perspectives in Psychotherapy and Inner Exploration.* State University of New York Press, New York, 1988.

Grosso M: *The Millennium Myth: Love and Death at the End of Time.* Quest, Wheaton, Illinois, 1995.

Hegel GW: *The Philosophy of Hegel.* Ed. CJ Friedrich. Modern Library, New York, 1953.

Henderson H. *Building a Win-Win World: Life Beyond Global Economics.* Barrett-Koehler, San Francisco, 1996.

Houston J: *Life-Force: The Psycho-Historical Recovery of the Self.* Delacorte, New York, 1980.

Hubbard BM: *The Evolutionary Journey: A Personal Guide to a Positive Future.* Evolutionary Press, San Rafael, California, 1982,
:*Conscious Evolution: Awakening the Power of Our Social Potential.* New World Library, Novato, California, 1998.

Ivanov-Smolensky AG: *Essays on the Pathophysiology of the Higher Nervous System,* Foreign Languages Publishing House, English ed., 1954. (Original   Russian ed. 1949/52.)

Jantsch E: *Design of Evolution: Self-Organization and Planning in the Life of Human Systems.* George Braziller, New York, 1975.

Laszlo E: *Evolution: The Grand Synthesis.* Shambhala, Boston and London, 1987.

Leonard GB: *The Transformation: A Guide to the Inevitable Changes in Humankind.* Delacorte Press, New York, 1972.

Lerner EJ: *The Big Bang Never Happened.* Vintage Books, Random House, New York, 1991/92.

Maslow AH: *The Further Reaches of Human Nature.* Penguin, New York, 1993.

McLaughlin C and Davidson G: *Spiritual Politics: Changing the World from the Inside Out.* Ballantine Books, New York, 1994.

Murphy M: *The Future of the Body: Explorations into the Further Evolution of Human Nature.* Jeremy P Tarcher, Los Angeles, 1992.

Needham J and Lu GD: *Celestial Lancets: A History & Rationale of Acupuncture & Moxa.* Cambridge University Press, Cambridge, England, 1980.

Needham J and Ronan CA: *The Shorter Science & Civilization in China.* Cambridge University Press, Cambridge, 1978.

Ornstein RF: *Multimind.* (Houghton Mifflin, Boston), 1986.
    : *The Right Mind: Making Sense of the Hemispheres.* Harcourt Brace, New York, 1997.

Pavlov IP: *Twenty Year of Objective Study of the Higher Nervous System Activity in Animals.* State Medical and Biological Publishing House, 1938.

Peck MS: *The Road Less Traveled and Beyond: Spiritual Growth in an Age of Anxiety.* Simon & Schuster, New York, 1997

Piaget J: *The Origin of Intelligence in Children* (trans. M Cook) WW Norton, 1963.
    : *The Grasp of Consciousness* (trans. S Wedgwood) Harvard Univ. Press, 1976.

Polak F: *The Image of the Future: The 21st Century and Beyond.* Prometheus Books, Buffalo, NY, 1976.

Pribram KH: "Toward a Holonomic Theory of Perception". In Ertel S (ed) *Gestalttheorie in der Modernen Psychologie.* Steinkopff, Darmstadt, Germany, 1975.
    : *Languages of the Brain: Experimental Paradoxes and Principles in Neuropsychology.* Brandon House, New York, 1982 and Erlbaull Assoc., Hillsdaly, NJ, 1990.

Rajneesh BS: *Tao – The Three Treasures: Talks on Fragments from Tao Te Ching by Lao Tzu, Vol. 1.* Rajneesh Foundation International, Rajneeshpuram, Oregon, 1976.
    : *Tao – The Three Treasures: Talks on Tao Tzu. Vol. 4.* Rajneesh Foundation, Poona, India, 1977.
    : *The Way of Tao: Discourses on Lao Tse's Tao-Te-King, Vol. 1* (Trans. Dolli Didi). Motilal Banarsidass, Delhi, India, 1978.
    : *The Way of Tao: Discourses on Lao Tse's Tao-Te-King, Vol. 2* (Trans. Dolli Didi) Motilal Banarsidass, Delhi, India, 1979.
    : *The New Man: The Only Hope for the Future.*

Rebel Publ House GmbH, Cologne, Germany, 1987.

Reich W: *Listen, Little Man!* (trans. R Manheim. Illus. W Steil) Farrar, Straus and Giroux, New York, 1948.
:*People in Trouble: The Emotional Plague of Mankind.* (trans. P Schmitz) Farrar, Straus and Giroux, New York, 1953.

Roszak TB: *The Voice of the Earth.* Simon & Schuster, New York, 1992.

Russell P: *The Global Brain Awakens: Our Next Evolutionary Leap.* Global Brain, Palo Alto, CA, 1995.

Sagan C: *Billions & Billions: Thoughts on Life and Death at the Brink of the Millennium.* Ballantine, 1997.

Sahtouris, E: *Gaia — The Human Journey from Chaos to Cosmos.* Pocket Books, New York & London, 1989.
: *Earth Dance: Living Systems in Evolution.* Metalog Books, Alameda, CA, 1995.

Salk J: *Anatomy of Reality: Merging of Intuition and Reason.* Columbia University Press, New York, 1983.

Sheldrake R: *A New Science of Life: The Hypothesis of Formative Causation.* JP Tarcher, Los Angeles, 1981.

Shlain L: *The Alphabet Versus the Goddess: The Conflict Between Word and Image.* Penguin, Middlesex, England/New York, 1998/99.

Sivik T and Schoenfeld R: "Somatization and the Paradigm of Psychosomatology". *Advances in Mind — Body Medicine* 2001; 17: 263-266.

Stock G: *Metaman: The Merging of Humans and Machines into a Global Superorganism.* Simon and Schuster, New York, 1993.

Talbot M: *The Holographic Universe.* HarperPerennial, New York, 1991.

Vygotsky LS: *Thought and Language.* A. Kozulin, ed. MIT Publ, Boston, 1986. (Original Russian edition, 1934).

Wilber K: *The Holographic Paradigm and Other Paradoxes: Exploring the Leading Edge of Science.* Shambhala, Boston & London, 1985.
: *Sex, Ecology, Spirituality: The Spirit of Evolution.* Shambhala, Boston & London, 1995.
: *A Brief History of Everything.* Shambhala, Boston & London, 1996.

Williamson M
: *A Return to Love.* HarperCollins, New York, 1996.

Yoo TW: *Koryo Sooji Chim.* Eum Yang Maek Jin Publ. Seoul, Korea, 1977 (in Korean) and *Koryo Hand Acupuncture.* P Eckman, Ed. 1988 (in English).

Young AM: *The Reflexive Universe: Evolution of Consciousness.* Delacorte, New York, 1976.

Zukav G: *The Seat of the Soul.* Simon & Schuster, New York, 1990.

1   There are two transliterations of Mandarin Chinese in current use: the older *Wade-Giles* and the more recent *Pinyin*. Although current publications generally utilize the *Pinyin*, most people are familiar with the Wade-Giles spelling of the title (*Tao Te Ching*) and the presumed author of this book (*Lao Tzu*) rather than the *Pinyin* (*Dao De Jing* by *Lao Zi*). Therefore in this case, and in all others where readers may be familiar with a name or word in the Wade-Giles spelling, I use this. In all other cases, I use the Pinyin spelling, often also giving the Wade-Giles in parenthesis.

2   Needham, the foremost western historian of the development of Chinese science from the earliest ancient times proposes that Lao Tzu lived in the 4th century BCE (Needham-Ronan, 1978, p 87).

3   First stanza of Verse 1.

4   For an explicit reference to Tao as the greatness of all entities and of the universe, see Verse 25.

5   According to Cheng 1981, p1.

6   See Schlain 1998.

7   From Verse 1.

8   Although purely non-confrontational modes may have been the best option for Lao Tzu's challenges to the establishment of his time, it is not to say that polemics and confrontational modes of action are not sometimes appropriate methods for us to facilitate change.

9   Our right cerebral hemisphere, according to psychophysiological findings of the past twenty-five years, functions as a more holistic consciousness, while the left hemisphere tends to be in charge of language-mediated rational (as well as rationalizing) thought. (See Gazzaniga 1973; Ornstein 1986; 1997; and Schlain 1998/99.) Pavlov referred to right brain consciousness as our *First Signaling System* and to left brain consciousness as our *Second Signaling System*. (See Pavlov 1938; and Ivanov-Smolensky 1954.) The physiological mediator and neurological "traffic director" for these two disparate functions is the corpus callosum, which connects the two cerebral hemispheres. It is important to understand the differentiation of left and right brain functions because Lao Tzu, without knowing about our split brain, implies, throughout the *Tao Te Ching*, that we can only walk the path toward the Great Integrity by releasing ourselves from our rationalizing prisons (left brain) and allowing our intuition (right brain) to play a greater role. See Table 1 in which I summarize the differentiations of the left and right cerebral hemispheres.

10 *Yin and Yang* is the ancient Chinese terminology for the concept that everything in our universe expresses itself in polarities; that is, in two fundamental contradictory as well as balancing forces (for example, active and passive, positive and negative, hot and cold) which both oppose and complement each other. The theory of polarities developed during the time of Lao Tzu, specifically in the Spring and Autumn Period (770-476 BCE during the Zhou (Chou) dynasty) (Dale 1993, p 82 and pp 247-249).

11 See Schlain 1998.

12 See the beginning of the *Preface* for Lao Tzu's five premises about the Great Integrity.

13 From Verse 15. For Lao Tzu, "ancient times" was the long period of tribal life that preceded civilization, and also perhaps the first thousand years of Chinese civilization, the legendary period between 4,000 and 2,500 BCE.

14 How can we know how it feels to be in the Great Integrity? Paradoxically, one way of acquiring a concrete image of a *future* non-toxic life style is by observing the past; for example, by studying some tribal peoples before they become physically, mentally, emotionally and spiritually corrupted by civilizations' uncivilized ways. A second way of acquiring a concrete image of a non-toxic life style is by observing the innocence of young children before they are corrupted.

15 From Rajneesh 1976, pp 272-273.

16 From Verse 15.

17 From Verse 2.

18 See Note 9 and Table 1.

19 See *Preface*, Note 12.

20 See Dale 1995.

21 See Dale 1968 (1 and 2).

22 See *Preface*, Note 13 for some of the numerous authors who are keen observers and activists of the transition to Epoch III, and who invite us to join them as conscious participants in the process.

23 That is, what Lao Tzu called the Tao (the Great Integrity). For us, the emergence of an integral consciousness requires our transcendence of the mechanistic and atomistic premises of Newtonian-Cartesian science, as well as the philosophical and theological premises of dualism.

24 From Verse 7.

25 Also see the Note in the Commentary on Verse 29.

26 See Table 2.

1 My translation of *Tao Te Ching* is *A Guide to the Theory and Practice of the Great Integrity*. See the beginning of the Introduction for a further explanation of how I arrived at this translation of the title.

2 See, for example, verses 1 and 54.

3 See Verse 25 for Lao Tzu's definition of the Tao. Taoism originates with Lao Tzu's concept of the Tao, and is further elucidated in the writings of Chuang-Tzu.

4 See, for example, Verse 4.

5 Ancient times, for the most part, were, for Lao Tzu, tribal societies that preceded civilization.

6 See, for example, verses 15, 39, 44, 52 and 65.

7 Modern sociologists refer to this antagonistic disassociation as *alienation*.

8 See, for example, verses 18 and 65.

9 See verses 1, 19, 37, 52, 55, 57, 60, and 72.

10 The early studies, beginning more than half a century ago include, among many others, the anthropological investigations of Margaret Mead, Ralph Linton and V. Gordon Childe, the sociological studies of Thorstein Veblen, Robert K. Merton, and Karl Mannheim, the historical studies of Joseph Needham, R.H. Tawney and George Thomson, the psychological studies of Jean Piaget, and the philosophical studies of Jean-Paul Sartre and Alfred North Whitehead.

11 From this point of view, the exodus from the Garden of Eden is more of a metaphor for our leaving the Great Integrity of tribal relations for the hostilities of civilizations than it is a parable about each of us being born in "original sin". As Lao Tzu points out, even in civilizations, we are all born innocent, and are only gradually conditioned to conform to the inhumanities of our institutions and social relations.

12 See, for example, Dexler et al 1991; and Stock 1993.

13 See, for example, Bateson 1979; Bohm/Weber 1985; Bohm 1980; Buck 1969; Caldicott 1992; Capra 1975/85; and 1982/88; Chaisson 1989; Csikszentmihalyi 1993; Dale 1968 (1 & 2); 1982; and 1995; Diamond 1997/99; Dossey 1982; Drexler et al 1991; Eisler 1987; Elgin 1993; Ferguson 1980/1987; Frankl 1985; Fuller 1991; Greene 1999; Grof 1988; Grosso 1995; Henderson 1996; Houston 1980; Hubbard 1982 and 1998; Jantsch 1975; Laszlo 1987; Leonard 1972; McLaughlin et al 1994; Murphy 1992; Peck 1997; Polak 1976; Rajneesh 1987; Roszak 1992; Sagan 1997; Sahtouris 1989; and 1995; Salk 1983; Sheldrake 1981; Stock 1993; Wilber 1995 and 1996; Williamson 1996; Young 1976 and Zukav 1990.

14 From Verse 20.

15 From Verse 8.

16 For example, the ear, hand, foot, scalp, iris, eye orbit, filtrum, lips, face, nose, back, abdomen, arms, legs, and neck. For a summary of these systems, see Dale 1999.

17 See, for example, Dale 1975; 1976 (1 & 2); 1984; 1985; and 1999.

18 That is to say that the order of the points within each system, for example, the ear, the hand or the foot, reiterates the anatomy of the body. In the hand, for example, the points relative to the upper part of the body such as the head are in the fingers (in Dr. Yoo's Korean hand system, the acupoints for the head are all localized in the distal joint of the middle finger), and the points relative to the lower parts of the body are in the lower palm area.

19 The micro-meridians of the *ear* were discovered by Chinese researchers (see *Auricular Acupuncture Therapy* 1972/74), and by Dr Frank R. Bahr (see Bahr 1999); the micro-meridians of the *hand* were discovered by Dr. Tae-Woo Yoo (see Yoo, ed. Eckman 1977/88); and the micro-meridians of the *foot*, were discovered in my own research (see Dale 1975; 1985).

20 Lao Tzu's Great Integrity thereby is the antithetical proposition to the main assumptions of western science based upon the theories of Descartes and Newton.

21 See Dale 1975; 1976 (1 & 2); 1984; 1985; and especially 1999.

22 See Sivik et al 2001.

23 See Pribram 1975; 1990.

24 See Bohm 1980; Bohm and Weber 1985; Wilber (ed) 1985; Capra 1975/85; and 1982/88. Also see Talbott 1991 as well as my commentary on Verse 42.

25 Cheng ms 1996.

26 Chi and Johnson ms 1997.

27 Richter 1998.

28 Star 2001.

29 See list of selected English editions.

1   See *Introduction*, Note 9 and Table 1, p.xiii.

2   The 10,000 phenomena is an ancient Chinese expression meaning all the different entities of the universe.

3   The main exception is modern physics (quantum and relativity theories). See Capra 1975/85; and 1982/88.

4   See Introduction, Note 10.

5   Also see verses 3 and 8.

6   See *Introduction*: Table 2, The Two Phases in the Development of Society and Consciousness and Their Synthesis in the Great Integrity.

7   Qi Gong (Chi Kung) is an ancient Chinese exercise that has recently been acquiring international popularity. There are many forms, but most of them involve special movement, concentration and breathing to balance and control the Vital Energy (Qi) of the body.

8   See *Introduction*, Note 9 and Table 1 for the differentiation of left and right brain functions.

9   See Verse 3.

10 See Verse 2.

11 See *Introduction*: The Three Aspects of Liberation. p.xiv-xv.

12 *Ten thousand* in this context means *endless*.

13 See Verse 41.

14 See W. Reich: *People in Trouble: The Emotional Plague of Mankind*, 1953; and *Listen, Little Man!*, 1948,

15 The first type of leader may also have existed during the earliest stage of Chinese civilization during the time of the three legendary emperors: Fu Xi (c. 4,000 BCE), Shen Nong (c. 3,000 BCE) and Huang Di (c. 2,500 BCE).

16 Also see verses 40, 41, 45, 78 and 81 for further elucidation on the question of paradox.

17 The Chinese word for great is *Tai* not *Tao*, so Lao Tzu is not referring to the literal meaning of *Tao*, but to its metaphorical character.

18 The last three lines of this last stanza beginning with "And the Great Integrity …", is an elaboration by the translation of Lao Tzu's short final line which simply states: *And the Tao is the great totality of nature.*

19 Bohm 1980, p. 174; Also see Bohm and Weber 1985; Dossey 1982; and Lerner 1991/92; as well as the Commentary on Verse 42.

20 See *Introduction* Table 2, p.xix.

21 Lao Tzu was the legendary archivist of King Ching who supposedly died in 520 BCE. According to the records, two of his sons, Prince Chao and Prince Ching battled each other to be his successor. First Chao was victorious. Then Ching overthrew his brother in 516 BCE. When Chao was banished, he took the royal archives with him. This same year, Confucius was supposed to have traveled from the state of Lu to the state of Chu to consult with Lao Tzu on matters of ritual. Confucius is said to have come out of the meeting denouncing Lao Tzu as a dragon. So being in the midst of political turmoil, having been robbed of his archives, being denounced by Confucius, and not having the spirit of a martyr, all seem reason enough for Lao Tzu to decide in middle age to retire to the mountains where he is supposed to have spent the rest of his life. Also see the commentary on Verse 38.

22 See Verse 68 and its commentary for a further amplification of these premises.

23 See Gazzaniga 1973; Ornstein 1986; and 1997; Shlain 1998/99; and Dale1995. Also see *Introduction*, Note 9 and Table 1. p.xiii.

24 Omnicide is John Somerville's term for the possible destruction of all life on our planet.

25 The literal translation of this last line is to "die without perishing" which I interpret to mean to leave a creative legacy for all future generations.

26 See Note 21.

27 See *Introduction* Note 9 and Table 1. Also see Verse 31 and its Commentary.

28 See Pavlov 1938; Ivanov-Smolensky 1954; and Vygotsky 1934/1936.

29 Also see Piaget 1963; and 1976.

30 That is, the topology of the micro-points and micro-channels reiterate the topology of the anatomy of the body and its Vital Energy patterns. See, for example, Dale 1975; 1976 [1 & 2]; 1984; 1985; and 1999.

31 See Karl Pribram 1975; 1990.

32 Sivik and Schoenfeld 2001.

33 See Bohm 1980; and Bohm and Weber 1985.

34 See Wilber 1985 and Talbot 1991. Also see the Commentary on Verse 25.

35 Hegel 1953 (English translation) and Gollobin 1986.

36 See *Introduction* Note 9 and Table 1 p.xvii; Also see the Commentary on Verse 41.

37 See Verse 1.

38 See Schlain, 1998: and Dale 1995.

39 See Verse 2.

40 To use the term *activities* instead of *actions* is to clarify Lao Tzu's frequent reminder that it is only without action that everything gets done. What he means by *action* is *coercive action*, that is, artificial and ego-satisfying intrusions into the rhythms of natural processes. He has no intention of suggesting that we all become vegetables, only that we accomplish our needs by learning to flow with processes rather than becoming their commanding outside agents.

41 Also see Commentaries on verses 15, 32 and 39.

42 For us, "this period" refers to the epoch of coercive civilizations. See *Introduction*, Table 2, p.xix.

43 See Commentary on Verse 67 The Three Treasures, p.257.

44 See Commentary on Verse 67.

45 Unfortunately, this characterization of life is still as true for us in the twenty-first century as it was for Lao Tzu and his contemporaries.

46 Richter 1998.

47 Star 2001.

48 See *Introduction* Note 10. Also see verses 5, 42, 45 and 77.

Index of Verse Titles